Development of the Knowledge Base for the

PRAXIS III: Classroom Performance Assessments Assessment Criteria

CAROL ANNE DWYER
Educational Testing Service

Educational Testing Service

TABLE OF CONTENTS

INTRODUCTION

This paper has two primary purposes: To provide an overview of the knowledge base that supports the criteria used in PRAXIS III: Classroom Performance Assessments and to provide an overview of the research and development process that was carried out to create and refine these criteria. This paper takes a retrospective, although not strictly chronological, approach to the description of the data collection, and is intended to give the reader an overview of a lengthy and complex research and development process. It serves as an introduction to, not as a complete description of, the main research activities that were carried out as part of PRAXIS III: Classroom Performance Assessments' development. Additional detail is provided in the Appendices to this paper, and the interested reader should consult the referenced original reports for complete technical and archival data.

It is expected that this report will be part of a dynamic process. As additional research findings that bear on PRAXIS III criteria cumulate, these must be considered along with the previous data in evaluating the continued importance of the criteria and the manner in which they are implemented in a wide range of classrooms.

PURPOSE AND NATURE OF PRAXIS III: CLASSROOM PERFORMANCE ASSESSMENTS

PRAXIS III: Classroom Performance Assessments of *THE PRAXIS SERIES: Professional Assessments for Beginning Teachers*® constitute a system for assessing the skills of beginning teachers in their own classroom settings. Another component of THE PRAXIS SERIES: Professional Assessments for Beginning Teachers®, the PRAXIS II: Subject Assessments, is intended to assess prospective teachers' depth and breadth of knowledge of subject matter and pedagogical principles, using a variety of problem formats. PRAXIS III is a complementary assessment; it does not aim to duplicate this assessment of subject-matter knowledge per se, although it assesses application of this knowledge in specific classroom settings.

Like the other parts of The PRAXIS Series: Professional Assessments for Beginning Teachers®, PRAXIS III was developed for use in beginning teacher licensing decisions made by states or local agencies empowered to license teachers. Under the policy guidelines that govern its use, PRAXIS III may *not* be used for the purpose of making employment decisions about teachers who are already licensed.

PRAXIS III is intended to be an assessment system that is open to public and professional scrutiny. Examination of the assessment criteria is especially encouraged. The PRAXIS III framework of knowledge and skills for beginning teachers, including the assessment criteria and scoring rules, as well as information about the assessment process itself, should be made available to all those who are involved in the use of PRAXIS III, particularly the beginning teachers who are to be assessed. It is hoped that the criteria can become part of the growing professional dialogue among teachers.

The PRAXIS III system uses three data-collection methods—direct observation of classroom practice, written descriptions of the students and what they are to learn, and interviews that are structured around the classroom observation. Prior to the observation, the beginning teacher provides the trained assessor with written documentation that conveys a sense of the general classroom context and the students in the class, as well as specific information about the lesson to be observed. Additional data collection occurs in semi-structured interviews before and after the observation, which allow for exploration of the teacher's rationales for his or her decisions and practices as well as an opportunity for reflection on

2

teaching practice. The interviews are also intended to assess the teacher's ability to relate instructional decisions to contextual factors such as student characteristics and prior knowledge.

PRAXIS III: Classroom Performance Assessments consist of three major components:

- the framework of knowledge and skills for beginning teachers used in PRAXIS III to assess teaching performance, including a set of assessment criteria and accompanying scoring rules that are designed to be used to gather data and make ratings at all grade levels and in all content areas

- the instruments and forms that trained assessors use to collect data (Class Profile, Instruction Profile, Preobservation Interview, Classroom Observation Record, and Postobservation Interview) and the form that the assessors use to analyze data, score the teaching performance for each criterion, and provide the rationale for their professional judgments (Record of Evidence)

- the training of assessors to document the teacher's performance and to accurately and reliably interpret and score the data they collect in a wide variety of classroom contexts.

The focus of this paper is on the development of the first of these three components, the assessment criteria, which are shown in Appendix A. Instruments and forms are provided in Appendix B. The assessor training is an intensive experience, organized into a five-day workshop with fieldwork and a culminating assessor proficiency test. An outline of a typical training session is provided in Appendix C. An overview of the assessment process and training is provided in Appendix D.

The framework of knowledge and skills whose development is described in this paper consists of four interrelated domains—Organizing Content Knowledge for Student Learning, Creating an Environment for Student Learning, Teaching for Student Learning, and Teacher Professionalism. The domains and their criteria are designed to be interrelated, not conceptually or statistically independent of each other, in order better to mirror the integrated nature of teaching itself. Each domain consists of a set of four or five criteria used to assess the teacher's performance; there are a total of 19 criteria in all. Each criterion represents a critical aspect of teaching, or lens through which teaching may be viewed, not a prescribed behavior or way to teach. The criteria are designed to allow a maximum amount of flexibility in how they may be demonstrated in various classroom contexts, and in accordance with a wide range of teaching styles. Another important characteristic of the PRAXIS III criteria is that, unlike assessment systems that limit attention to issues of equity and diversity to a single criterion or a small subset of these, PRAXIS III has infused a multicultural perspective throughout the system. This perspective is based on the premise that effective teaching requires familiarity with students' background knowledge and experiences (including their cultural resources), and effective teachers use this familiarity to devise appropriate instruction (see Dwyer, 1993; Dwyer & Villegas, 1993; and Rodriguez, Sjostrom, & Villegas, 1993, for fuller discussions of this point).

The knowledge base that underlies the development of these PRAXIS III assessment criteria is the subject of the remainder of this paper.

Development of the Knowledge Base

In developing PRAXIS III: Classroom Performance Assessments, it was necessary to articulate both a guiding conception of teaching and learning (a core values statement) and a set of criteria by which beginning teaching could be assessed. The conception of teaching and learning that is the touchstone for PRAXIS III development is described elsewhere (Dwyer and Villegas, 1993). This guiding conception makes clear the most basic principles that guided the PRAXIS III research and development effort (see also Dwyer, 1991, 1993). These include the assumption that effective teaching requires both action and decision making and that learning is a process of the active construction of knowledge. The guiding conception also makes explicit the belief that because good teaching is dependent on the subject matter and the students, assessments should not attempt to dictate a teaching method or style that is to be applied in all contexts.

The developers of PRAXIS III derived the base of knowledge from which the first operational form of the assessment criteria was produced over a lengthy development period (1987-1993). It is expected that further information bearing on these criteria will emerge from data on those who will now use PRAXIS III: Classroom Performance Assessments for decision making about beginning teachers, as well as from more basic educational and psychological research.

The intent of the developers of PRAXIS III: Classroom Performance Assessments was to amass and synthesize the knowledge base for teaching, as it is represented from three perspectives: practicing teachers' knowledge; the theory and data developed by educational researchers; and the requirements developed by state teacher licensing authorities. These are, of course, interrelated sources of knowledge. Teaching practice draws to a certain extent on educational theory, for example, and state teacher licensing authorities typically derive their requirements from this same pool of research, through the participation of teacher educators and other educational researchers in setting these requirements. Each of these three sources of data will be described in more detail in a later section of this paper.

The intent of Educational Testing Service and the PRAXIS III staff with respect to the knowledge-base activities was, from the inception of the project, to be descriptive rather than prescriptive. The role of the

PRAXIS III: Classroom Performance Assessments developers has been to identify, through a wide variety of methodologies, a national consensus on important aspects of teaching and to translate the substance of this consensus into terms that are useful both for decision making for licensing beginning teachers and for those beginning teachers' own professional development. There were no *a priori* constraints imposed on the form or scope of the data gathering to establish the knowledge base; no predetermined method for gathering evidence about the criteria; and no pre-set number of criteria or framework for their organization. The resulting criteria should thus *not* be considered "the ETS view" of teaching, but the view that the PRAXIS III staff have deduced from working closely with teachers themselves, and a view that is informed by the theoretical and policy perspectives of other educators and researchers. As these criteria are used in various settings, and as additional research is carried out, it is expected that there will be a continuing need to update and refine the assessment criteria.

CONCEPTUAL DILEMMAS
IN THE KNOWLEDGE BASE

The developers of the PRAXIS III: Classroom Performance Assessments encountered a number of true dilemmas as the knowledge-base building process unfolded. These dilemmas did not yield to simple solutions and were of differing types.

First, there is the basic question, "From whose perspective should the knowledge base be considered?" As noted above, our three main sources of data for the knowledge base were practicing teachers, the research/theoretical perspective, and teacher licensing requirements. Each of these perspectives does not simply provide a different view of the same phenomena; each asks different questions, employs differing methods to reach conclusions, and has a set of different, although often related, concerns about the meaning and use of knowledge about teaching. These three views represent fundamentally different paradigms, in the sense that basic assumptions, methodologies, and values differ. It is therefore not an algorithmic or mechanical process to arrive at criteria that incorporate data from these three sources. The developers of PRAXIS III carried out an iterative procedure of creating draft criteria, then presenting them for review to representatives of these three main points of view. (See Figure 1 for a schematic representation of the process, which is discussed in greater detail in a later section of this paper.) Reviewers and panelists were asked, in essence, if the draft criteria represented the knowledge base for teaching as they understood it. As shown in Appendix E, the criteria underwent a number of major revisions as a result of this process. With each of these major revisions, increasingly large cycles of fieldwork were undertaken.

As data from the fieldwork accumulated, such practical considerations as whether those who assess the beginning teachers could understand what was meant by a particular criterion came into play in evaluating the criteria. In addition, because the PRAXIS III: Classroom Performance Assessments are intended to improve teaching practice as well as to aid decision makers, recognizability and acceptability to the teaching profession (see Gage, 1974, for a discussion of this relationship) were explicitly used in judging the merits of the later versions of the PRAXIS III assessment criteria. This focus on improving teaching practice is also germane to establishing the consequential basis for the validity of the assessments

(Messick, 1992): The assessments should contribute to the improvement of the educational system of which they are a part.

In the end, of course, no matter how they were arrived at, the criteria must be judged on their own merits by each person who reads them, using the evaluative standards that are part of his or her own personal and professional world view. It is very likely, however, that the standards used to evaluate the PRAXIS III assessment criteria will include the broad set of requirements that the National Board for Professional Teaching Standards has for its assessments: "The assessments must be professionally credible, publicly acceptable, legally defensible, administratively feasible, and economically affordable" (National Board for Professional Teaching Standards, 1991, p. 53).

Another related dilemma faced by the developers of the PRAXIS III: Classroom Performance Assessments was the relative standing of theoretical and practical knowledge. Sternberg and Wagner (1993) draw a useful distinction between academic problems and practical problems. Academic problems tend to (a) be formulated by other people, (b) be well-defined, (c) be complete with regard to the information needed to solve them, (d) possess only a single correct answer, (e) possess only a single method of obtaining the correct answer, (f) not be embedded in ordinary experience, and (g) be of little or no intrinsic interest. In contrast, according to Sternberg and Wagner, practical problems tend to (a) require problem recognition and formulation, (b) be ill-defined, (c) require information seeking, (d) possess multiple acceptable solutions, (e) allow multiple paths to solution, (f) be embedded in and require prior everyday experience, and (g) require motivation and personal involvement (p. 2). It is clear that in Sternberg and Wagner's terms PRAXIS III addresses the practical problems that beginning teachers must solve. As noted above, it is important for both practical and theoretical reasons that the criteria and their organizing framework map well to teachers' own understandings of their work. At the same time, however, the criteria should also build on educational and psychological theory, in order to give them coherence and generalizability, as well as an increased probability of standing the test of time in actual classroom use. Again, resolving this dilemma was not a mechanistic process. Many practicing teachers and educational theoreticians reviewed and helped to revise the criteria until they were broadly perceived as acceptable from both points of view.

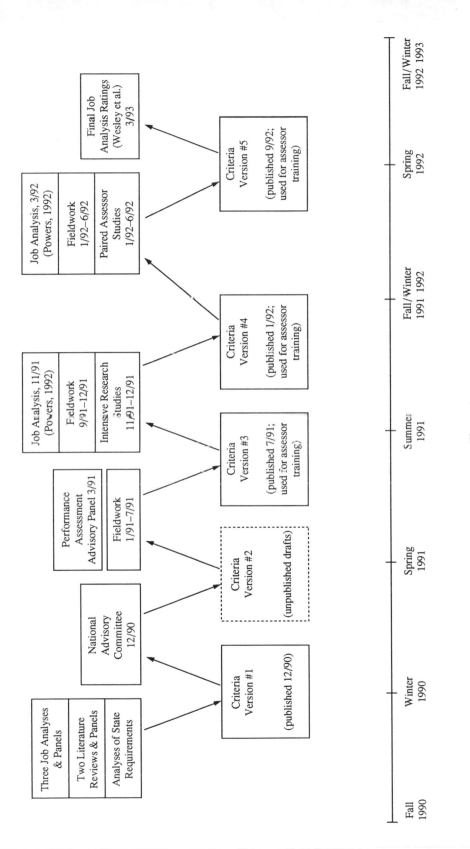

Figure 1
Criteria Development Schematic

The developers of the PRAXIS III: Classroom Performance Assessments criteria were also faced with what is often called the "lead/lag" dilemma. As part of the system for licensing beginning teachers, the criteria must reflect currently acceptable professional practice in order to be logically consistent with the purposes of the assessments and fair to the participants. A competing value, however, is that given the long lead time for developing high-quality assessments, and the likelihood that they will continue to be used for a number of years, it is also important not to create assessments that will be, in effect, obsolete before they are completed, or that will encourage continuation of teaching practices that are even now only marginally acceptable to the profession. The crux of this dilemma is that currently acceptable professional practice is by no means a static concept, and that new knowledge about teaching is created on a daily basis. In evaluating whether a particular aspect of teaching can be considered to be supported by research, it is thus necessary to make a number of complex judgments about the status of the research and to take into consideration the professional consensus about future trends in that area. It is also necessary to include in these deliberations some judgments about the definitiveness of a research area. For example, the area of teacher behavior and its links to student learning has been extensively researched for many years. In particular subareas, the domains are well mapped, well-designed studies are numerous, and it is even possible to say that definitive conclusions have been reached. In contrast, the area of teacher cognition and its links to student learning is still relatively young and in a state of flux. Although the importance of this research domain to teaching practice is not in dispute, its contours are still to a certain extent under discussion, and a number of important principles, although logically unassailable and convincingly demonstrated in high-quality research studies, have not yet been widely replicated, and their interconnections are not yet fully established. A complicating factor is that research on teacher behavior and research on teacher cognition tend to utilize different research methodologies, thus creating another difficulty in evaluating the newer research by traditional standards. Despite these conceptual difficulties, and despite the fact that teacher cognition has not heretofore been successfully addressed in teacher assessments, it is clear that the PRAXIS III: Classroom Performance Assessments would have very little credibility among teachers and other educators and researchers, now and in the future, if this perspective were to be ignored.

SCOPE OF THE CRITERIA

Two interrelated issues that might be characterized as issues related to the scope of the criteria were addressed by the PRAXIS III developers in the process of translating the knowledge base into specific criteria: Finding the appropriate "size" or level of generality for the criteria; and determining the range of teaching contexts to which the criteria apply.

The enormous variability among classroom contexts (Shulman, 1988a, 1988b; Stodolsky, 1988) poses significant challenges for any assessment effort. In the case of the PRAXIS III: Classroom Performance Assessments, the teaching criteria have been designed as principles to be applied in a wide range of teaching contexts (including variability in subject matter and grade level taught, teaching style, and students' individual and background characteristics) rather than as specific "rules" to be followed or behaviors to be demonstrated. A major issue in being able to design practical assessments that can accommodate a wide range of contexts has been getting to the right size of concept for the criteria. Some researchers (Kagan, 1990; Katz and Raths, 1985) have called this challenge the "Goldilocks Principle." In the PRAXIS III: Classroom Performance Assessments, this principle means that if the criteria are too big, that is, too vague and general, then meaningful standards are difficult to develop and to apply fairly; assessors cannot bring a consistent set of judgments to the assessment process. On the other hand, if criteria are too small, that is, too specific, they can be judged with great consistency, but they will not capture the essence of good teaching and may promote a fragmented, cookbook approach to teaching. Thus, the assessment criteria, like the bears' porridge that Goldilocks tasted, must be "just right," if they are to meet the goals of fair assessment and improvement of teaching practice. Finding the level of specificity that is "just right" involves many iterations of fieldwork and analysis. In the reports of this fieldwork, there are numerous instances of these experiences leading the developers to conclude, for example, that what had been a single criterion ought to be divided into two separate criteria to help assessors better understand how a particular aspect of teaching is actually played out in the classroom and help them recognize evidence related to this aspect of teaching when they see it (Myford, Villegas, Reynolds, Camp, Jones, Knapp, Mandinach, Morris, & Sjostrom, 1993). The fieldwork also enabled the assessors and developers to see how the criteria related to each other in practice, and to use this information as the basis for making changes in how the criteria are organized, ordered, and described. Organizing and wording the criteria so that they are clear and logical from the point of view of those who use them was given a high priority in the development work.

In the fieldwork, there was also an opportunity to test the applicability of the criteria to a wide range of teaching contexts. The fieldwork was a rich source of the numerous examples of the criteria (in different subject matters, at different grade levels, etc.) that are needed to train assessors to recognize positive and negative instances of the criteria under very different circumstances.

Three Main Elements
of the Knowledge Base

Analyses of Important Tasks for Beginning Teachers

A series of formal analyses of the important tasks required of beginning teaching (often called job analyses) was carried out as part of the development of the PRAXIS III: Classroom Performance Assessments. Teachers and others familiar with their work were asked about the importance of various elements of the work of beginning teachers. This methodology provides an excellent overview of current practice as it is perceived by those working most closely with it and encourages respondents to make suggestions about other aspects of teaching that they consider important. There were three distinct stages of job analysis for PRAXIS III, each of which built upon its predecessors: (a) large-scale studies at the very beginning of the project; (b) a smaller study when the first major round of fieldwork was completed and analyzed, and the criteria revised on the basis of it; and (c) a study of the final developmental form of the criteria, after revisions had been made based on all of the fieldwork.

The first studies (Rosenfeld, Freeberg, & Bukatko, 1992; Rosenfeld, Reynolds, & Bukatko, 1992; Rosenfeld, Wilder, & Bukatko, 1992), although necessarily preliminary in nature because they preceded any assessment development, are large-scale, extremely thorough surveys of the knowledge and skills needed by beginning teachers, as evidenced by the activities they perform. The job analysis process was carried out separately for elementary school, middle school, and secondary school teachers. The content of these surveys was developed by numerous local, regional, and national panels of teachers and other educators, aided by PRAXIS III staff and the following associations: The American Association of Colleges for Teacher Education, the American Federation of Teachers, the National Association of Elementary School Principals, the National Association of Secondary School Principals, the National Association of State Directors of Teacher Education and Certification, and the National Education Association. Thousands of respondents were asked in detail about the importance of specific tasks for their own teaching, and for that of beginning teachers. Respondents were also asked to suggest other important aspects of teaching that might not have been represented in the surveys. The very specific task statements were used to construct the more comprehensive assessment criteria. The results of these surveys thus formed an important part of the knowledge base for the first set of experimental criteria. A significant outcome of these initial studies was the high degree of similarity of results across different groups doing the rating, and across grade level and subject-matter taught. This finding, later reinforced by evidence from the field studies, was highly influential in the decision to create a single set of criteria to be used in assessing different grade levels and subjects taught. After this initial series of studies, work proceeded on a unified set of criteria that were designed not to require specific behaviors of the beginning teacher, but to identify important aspects of teaching that have validity in a wide variety of contexts.

In the next two job analysis studies, the criteria themselves had been developed and field-tested and were thus available to be evaluated directly. In the first of these two studies, when the criteria had been refined through fieldwork and tested in actual classrooms, two multi-state samples of teachers and other educators were asked to rate the actual criteria (Powers, 1992.) In the fall of 1991, a sample of 114 teachers and teacher educators rated a preliminary version of the criteria (July 1991 version; see Figure 1). A majority of this sample were elementary-level teachers. In the spring of 1992, a second sample of 131 educators, comprised mainly of secondary-level teachers who were licensed in one or more subject areas, rated the importance of a revised set of criteria (January 1992 version; see Figure 1). In this study, participants were given the criteria and brief explanations of them, and were then asked to rate the importance of these criteria to the job of the beginning teacher. Although some differences were noted among the criteria in this study, there was a high degree of endorsement of each of these two versions of the criteria as being important to the job of the beginning teacher.

Finally, following availability of all field test data and all resultant revisions to the criteria in the fall of 1992, the last version of the criteria was again rated for importance by a national sample of teachers (Wesley, Rosenfeld, & Sims-Gunzenhauser, 1993). Like the Powers (1992) study, this study was designed to build on the others before it. Because the Wesley et al. study directly assessed whether the long chain of development steps and input from different professional perspectives had indeed resulted in assessment criteria that are important to the job of the beginning teacher, this overview paper concentrates on these, rather than on the earlier formative data. Full details of the earlier studies are provided in the reports referenced above.

Research and Theoretical Perspectives

In order to supplement the views obtained by the job analysis methodology described above, research and theoretical perspectives were directly incorporated into the knowledge base by a series of research reviews. These reviews strengthen the professional basis of the assessments by documenting what is known both empirically and theoretically about good practice for teachers in general, and for beginning teachers in particular. Early in the development process, building on existing research reviews such as Wittrock (1985), special literature reviews were commissioned on effective teaching, effective beginning teaching, and effective teaching in multicultural classrooms (publication versions of these reviews can be found in Reynolds, 1992, and Villegas, 1992). These efforts were undertaken by ETS researchers, working closely with panels of eminent researchers from other institutions (see Appendix F for lists of panel members). Jones (1992) provided an update and interpretation of these reviews organized in terms of the set of assessment criteria that were used in the spring 1992 fieldwork.

The current overview uses these sources as a basis, with additional recent studies, to provide highlights of particularly significant research related to each of the 19 PRAXIS III: Classroom Performance Assessments criteria.

Analyses of State Regulations for Teacher Licensing

During the past decade, a number of states have adopted performance assessment systems for beginning teachers. The work of these states was an important supplementary source of information in the development of PRAXIS III: Classroom Performance Assessments. Analyses of states' regulations and practices necessarily included attention to both content and methodology. Comprehensive national analyses were undertaken to identify and compile information on the teacher licensing requirements in all 50 states and the District of Columbia. A subset of this information dealt with requirements related to assessment of actual teaching, rather than other knowledge, skill, experience, or educational attainment requirements. It is this subset related to assessment of actual teaching that formed the basis of the information collected for the development of the PRAXIS III: Classroom Performance Assessments. Building on earlier work done in the states themselves (e.g., Logan, Garland, & Ellett, 1989), a nationwide content analysis of state performance assessment requirements was carried out (Street, 1991) early in the development of PRAXIS III. This content analysis was designed to determine the content overlap among the systems and to isolate the distinctive differences among them. This study revealed a great deal of consistency among the states using classroom performance assessments in terms of what was being measured, although this content was often organized very differently in different states. State systems were also very different from one another in terms of the level of specificity with which they described a particular aspect of teaching. (Kuligowski, Holdzkom, and French have also provided a recent study [1993] of southeastern states that is generally consistent with these findings.)

Given that most of the states performance assessment systems analyzed were developed 10 or more years ago, it is perhaps not surprising that (with a few exceptions) they dealt almost exclusively with teacher behavior, and did not give systematic attention to teacher cognition. A recently published study by Tracy and Smeaton (1993), whose data are contemporaneous with those of Street (1991) and Klem (1993), reached remarkably similar conclusions about the consistency of content being measured by state teacher performance assessments. In states with criteria stated rather generally, Tracy and Smeaton cite the three most-measured areas as being instructional skills, classroom management, and interpersonal relationships (p. 224). In the PRAXIS III: Classroom Performance Assessments, these correspond closely to Domain B (Creating an environment for student learning) and Domain C (Teaching for student learning). In states with criteria stated at a more detailed level, Tracy and Smeaton cite nine criteria measured by at least two-thirds of the states in their analysis (p. 225). These are shown below with the domains or criteria of PRAXIS III that correspond most closely to them.

Tracy & Smeaton Summary of Nine Most Frequent State Criteria	PRAXIS III: Classroom Performance Assessments Domains and Criteria
1) Instructional planning and preparation	Domain A: Organizing content for student learning (all)
2) Management of class time	C5: Using instructional time effectively
3) Maintenance of classroom climate conducive to learning	Domain B: Creating an Environment for Student Learning (all)
4) Use of instructional materials	A4: Creating or selecting teaching methods, learning activities, and instructional materials or other resources that are appropriate for the students and that are aligned with the goals of the lesson
5) Student practice and application	C4: Monitoring students' understanding of content through a variety of means, providing feedback to students to assist learning, and adjusting learning activities as the situation demands C5: Using instructional time effectively
6) Monitoring and feedback of student progress	C4: Monitoring students' understanding of content through a variety of means, providing feedback to students to assist learning, and adjusting learning activities as the situation demands

Tracy & Smeaton Summary of Nine Most Frequent State Criteria	PRAXIS III: Classroom Performance Assessments Domains and Criteria
7) Evaluation of student progress	A5: Creating or selecting evaluation strategies that are appropriate for the students and that are aligned with the goals of the lesson C4: Monitoring students' understanding of content through a variety of means, providing feedback to students to assist learning, and adjusting learning activities as the situation demands
8) Critical thinking and problem solving	C3: Encouraging students to extend their thinking
9) Addressing individual student differences	A1: Becoming familiar with relevant aspects of students' background knowledge and experiences A2: Articulating clear learning goals for the lesson that are appropriate for the students A4: Creating or selecting teaching methods, learning activities, and instructional materials or other resources that are appropriate for the students and that are aligned with the goals of the lesson A5: Creating or selecting evaluation strategies that are appropriate for the lesson B1: Creating a climate that promotes fairness C2: Making content comprehensible to students

Because states' assessment practices are subject to considerable variation over time, it is difficult to provide detailed and up-to-date data on their content and methodology (Klem, 1990). With the help of an annually revised computer data base, it is possible to give the current status as of the writing of this overview, but that certainly does not guarantee that it will remain current, even in the short term. Klem's 1993 data form the basis of the commentary in this overview for each of the criteria.

THE PROCESS OF DEVELOPING THE CRITERIA

The job analyses, literature reviews, and state requirements, activities, and studies described above were embedded in a larger context of field consultation and research. As noted above, the separate studies were examined for similarities and differences among the perspectives provided by the practicing educators, researchers, and the states. These studies enabled the developers of the PRAXIS III: Classroom Performance Assessments to draft an initial set of assessment criteria derived from this research base. These reports and the draft criteria were presented to a National Advisory Committee (see Appendix G for membership list) that met in December 1990 to review the research base and the draft assessment criteria, and to provide specific input to the development process. The National Advisory Committee reacted favorably to the work done up to that point, including the elements of the knowledge base itself, and its initial translation into criteria, but advised the development team to articulate the guiding conception of teaching more fully and to bring the criteria more closely into line with this conception and its implications for interpreting the research base. The thrust of the committee's advice at this point was that the framework and mode of expression of the criteria did not accurately represent some important underlying concepts in the research base, in that the language and organization of the framework and criteria were more traditionally academic than the current purposes and state of knowledge warranted.

At this point in the development process, ETS researchers and developers pilot tested several revised versions of the criteria and the assessment process on a small scale in New Jersey, Pennsylvania, and California in preparation for larger-scale collaborative pilot studies with states. Concurrently, ETS sought collaborations with a small number of states with similar ideals and goals for assessing beginning teachers for licensure. Delaware and Minnesota were selected as initial partners in development of the PRAXIS III: Classroom Performance Assessments (Austria, 1993; Wilkins, 1993). Because of slight differences in the schedule of reaching formal agreement with ETS on the terms of these collaborations, beginning work with Delaware preceded beginning work with Minnesota by approximately three months.

In the spring of 1991, ETS researchers, working with a group of experienced teachers in Delaware, piloted the criteria and assessment process with student teachers in Delaware. Input from this experience was used to refine and further shape the criteria and assessment system. In June 1991, the initial group of collaborating experienced teachers from Delaware met with ETS research and development staff and a group of experienced teachers from Minnesota for intensive review and revision of the criteria, the assessment process, and the draft data collection instruments. During this critical stage of development, emphasis was placed on the application of the criteria in actual classrooms, and the need for the entire assessment process, including the criteria, to be accessible to both beginning and experienced teachers. The collaborating teachers worked with ETS staff to translate research-based concepts into criteria that could be used in a wide variety of classrooms, that would be well understood by both the assessors and the candidates, and would be useful in giving feedback to the beginning teacher. ETS staff and the collaborating teachers needed to accomplish all of this while maintaining the integrity of the underlying concepts from the point of view of the job requirements of the beginning teacher, from a research and theoretical point of view, and with respect to states' licensing requirements.

Input from these experienced teachers and the small-scale pilot-testing experience resulted in extensive changes to the criteria and their framework; the data collection instruments; the assessment process itself; and the design and content of the assessor training program. The next official version of the criteria was published in July 1991 in preparation for training assessors in Delaware and Minnesota and conducting larger-scale fieldwork in those two states in fall 1991. Before this larger-scale fieldwork began, additional experience was gained during the summer of 1991 in a program for at-risk students in Louisiana. This phase of the research process was carried out by a team of Delaware teachers and ETS staff, and highlighted the need for specific verbal descriptions of levels of performance (scoring rules) for each of the criteria in the framework, which had not existed up to this point. Scoring rules for each of the criteria were drafted, and then reviewed by the initial group of Delaware and Minnesota collaborating teachers and by other consulting teachers and researchers. Refinements were made to the scoring rules and the score scale as a result of this input. The criteria and scoring rules, data collection forms, and assessor training materials were then finalized for the first large-scale field studies, which took place in Delaware and Minnesota in the fall of 1991. The revised (July 1991) set of criteria and descriptions and scoring rules as they were used in these field studies can be found in Appendix E.

The fall 1991 field studies began with the training of assessors in Delaware and Minnesota to implement the assessment process in schools in the state (those being assessed, the "candidates," were student teachers in Delaware and first-year teachers in Minnesota). Along with the assessor training and data collection that took place in each state, research studies were also conducted to analyze in detail each component of the assessment system. The research studies, utilizing both quantitative and qualitative methodologies, were intended to provide information about changes that were needed in the criteria and framework, the data collection instruments, and the assessor training program (Myford et al., 1993). This research was conducted in a series of eight related studies conducted in three intensive research cycles in Delaware and Minnesota in fall 1991, with a research team composed of equal numbers of teachers and ETS research and development staff. As a result of this field work and analysis, extensive refinements to nearly every aspect of the assessment process were identified and implemented. Myford et al. (1993) show the wide range of topics addressed by this work. For example, this series of studies resulted in: changing the structure of the assessor training in order to eliminate common sources of confusion about particular criteria and scoring rules; changing the instructions to the assessors about how to take effective notes and code them for later use; understanding how assessors utilize multiple pieces of evidence regarding the same criterion; and pin-pointing which of the criteria needed changes in wording, organization, etc., in order to mirror actual teaching practice effectively.

These changes were implemented immediately and incorporated into the materials and procedures used in the spring 1992 field studies in Delaware and Minnesota, and the spring 1992 training that was carried out to support this effort. The version of the criteria that was published in January 1992 (see Appendix E) was the result of this phase of research and development. This version was used in the training of additional assessors in Delaware and Minnesota for data collection in the spring of 1992. In spring 1992, both the "veteran" and the newly trained assessors in Delaware and Minnesota field-tested the revised instruments, criteria, and scoring rules. The spring 1992 data-collection effort focussed on collection of paired ratings of the criteria. Wherever possible, assessors conducted their observations independently but with the same beginning teacher during the same lesson, so that the resulting ratings could later be compared. Interviews were conducted by one member of the pair, but each assessor made independent notes about the interview. Individual (single-assessor) ratings were also collected when pairs of assessors could not be formed. In both waves of field testing, extensive debriefings with the experienced teachers who served as assessors and with the student and beginning teachers who were being assessed served as an additional source of data for revision of the criteria, instruments, and procedures.

The results of this fieldwork formed the basis for finalizing the assessments available for initial use and inspection by states considering their adoption for teacher licensing in fall 1992. This final set of developmental criteria, along with descriptions and scoring rules, is found in Appendix A.

The remainder of this report is organized by the framework of four domains and 19 criteria. Each of the domains is named and described, then each criterion is given and described. For each of the criteria, information is given about the three main knowledge base elements (related research literature, related job analysis findings, related state licensing requirements) and relevant fieldwork findings.

DOMAIN A: ORGANIZING CONTENT KNOWLEDGE FOR STUDENT LEARNING

Knowledge of the content to be taught underlies all aspects of good instruction. Domain A focuses on how teachers use their understanding of students and subject matter to decide on learning goals; to design or select appropriate activities and instructional materials; to sequence instruction in ways that will help students to meet short- and long-term curricular goals; and to design or select informative evaluation strategies. All of these processes, beginning with the learning goals, must be aligned with each other, and because of the diverse needs represented in any class, each of the processes mentioned must be carried out in ways that take into account the variety of knowledge and experiences that students bring to class. Therefore, knowledge of relevant information about the students themselves is an integral part of this domain.

Domain A is concerned with how the teacher thinks about the content to be taught. This thinking is evident in how the teacher organizes instruction for the benefit of her or his students.

Domain A consists of the following five criteria.

Criterion A1: Becoming Familiar With Relevant Aspects of Students' Background Knowledge and Experiences

CRITERION DESCRIPTION. Research in cognitive science shows that students learn not simply by memorizing facts, but by reconfiguring and reorganizing what they already know. This means that students' experiences, both individual and cultural, are the essential material for learning. Teaching entails building bridges between the content to be learned and students' background knowledge and experiences. Therefore, teachers must become aware of these experiences.

Background knowledge and experiences include students' prior knowledge of the subject, their skills, interests, motivation to learn, developmental levels, and cultural experiences. Gaining information about some of these factors, such as prior knowledge or skills related to the content, may be relatively straightforward; for example, pretesting on the content to be taught can be a useful tool for the teacher. Less formal means, such as classroom discussion or observation of students, can contribute information not only about students' prior knowledge, but also about their interests, motivation, development levels, and cultural resources. Students as individuals differ with respect to any or all of these factors. Culturally, students differ in their beliefs, values, and ways of relating to the world. In classrooms, these cultural differences are manifested in how the students interact with each other and with the teacher, how they use language, how they approach learning tasks, and how they demonstrate what they know, among other things.

"Cultural differences" or "cultural diversity" are broadly defined to include ethnic differences, other differences associated with language group, socioeconomic background, and exceptionalities, as well as gender. To the extent possible, teachers should become familiar with and sensitive to the background experiences of students in these groups in order to build on students' experiences during instruction. However, group membership should never be used as a basis for stereotypical judgments about students.

Although teachers need knowledge of cultural differences, it would be unrealistic and impractical to expect beginning teachers to have a thorough understanding of the numerous cultural groups in our society. They should know, however, various procedures through which they can gain information about those communities that are represented in their classes. These procedures may include making home visits, conferring with community members, talking with parents, consulting with more-experienced colleagues, and observing children in and out of school to discern patterns of behavior that may be related to their cultural backgrounds.

The extent to which it is possible for teachers to become familiar with the various aspects of individual students' background knowledge and experiences may be affected by many factors, such as the number of students in the classroom and the amount of time each day that the teacher spends with a particular group. Teachers in self-contained classrooms, for example, may be expected to learn a great deal about their students' backgrounds and experiences. In some situations, such as a schedule and teaching load that assigns hundreds of students to one teacher, the teacher may be able to gain only a general understanding of the backgrounds of the students as a group. Regardless of their teaching assignment, however, all teachers need to know various procedures by which they can become familiar with their students' backgrounds and experiences.

As teachers gain skill, their understanding of the importance of gaining such information should deepen, and their knowledge of appropriate ways of gaining it should broaden.

Related Research Literature

Becoming familiar with, and building on, students' existing knowledge and experiences is the cornerstone of effective teaching practice for students of all backgrounds. According to Sykes and Bird (1992), "There has been an explosion of research [on students' prior knowledge] around children's conceptions of mathematics, of scientific concepts— of school knowledge and skills in general. This work strongly demonstrates that prior conceptions exert a powerful hold and are difficult to alter. Contemporary instructional aims include inducing conceptual change as a central preoccupation" (p. 28). This important fact relates both to this criterion and to Criterion C2 ("Making content comprehensible to students"): In Criterion A1, the emphasis is on learning about students' backgrounds and experiences; in Criterion C2, the emphasis is on using this knowledge in the act of teaching.

Recognition and implementation of this constructivist point of view is a major mechanism for ensuring equitable teaching of students of all backgrounds, in what Villegas (1991, 1992) and others have called "culturally responsive teaching." Building on the work of Cazden and Mehan (1989), Delpit (1988), Diaz, Moll, and Mehan (1986), Gallimore (1985), Heath (1983), Hollins (1989), Moll (1988), and Wong-Fillmore (1990), Villegas (1992) concludes that students from a wide variety of cultural backgrounds can come to learn about and profit from the culture of the classroom by building on students' cultural resources (p. 7). This entails extending the core concept of building on students' prior knowledge, the essence of good teaching, to students of all cultural backgrounds.

The influential U.S. Department of Education report, *What Works* (1987), listed 59 effective educational practices drawn from contemporary research and from opinions of distinguished thinkers, where these opinions have been documented as having achieved professional consensus. *What Works* included among these most effective practices the need to help students relate prior knowledge to new facts and concepts. Shulman (1987) helps us understand why this is such a critical practice and how it can be implemented in the classroom: "Adaptation is the process of fitting the represented material to the characteristics of the students. What are the relevant aspects of student ability, gender, language, culture, motivations, or prior knowledge and skills that will affect their responses to different forms of representation and presentation? What student conceptions, misconceptions, expectations, motives, difficulties, or strategies might influence the ways in which they approach, interpret, understand, or misunderstand the material? Related to adaptation is tailoring, which refers to the fitting of the material to the specific students in one's classrooms rather than to students in general" (p. 17). Shulman also cites knowledge of learners and their characteristics as one of the seven constituent knowledge elements for good teaching.

Glaser (1984) and Floden (1991), among others, detail the roots of conclusions such as these in schema theory.

Jones (1992) has summarized research indicating that students differ in a variety of domains such as cognitive, affective, physical, cultural, and experiential factors, which affect their response to specific instruction.

In contrast to experienced teachers, beginning teachers often view these student differences as problematic and are less apt to consider prior knowledge and experience in their planning (Carter, Cushing, Sabers, Stein & Berliner, 1988; Fogarty, Wang & Creek, 1983; Paine, 1989; Pinnegar, 1989; Reynolds, 1992; Shulman, 1989). However, this transition must be accomplished in order for learning to occur. Teachers need to understand the factors that have shaped the ways in which the student makes sense of the world (Cazden, 1986; Corno & Snow, 1986; Heath, 1983; Hilliard, 1989; Vosniadou, 1992). A student's prior knowledge influences the processing of new information either in a facilitative or a dysfunctional sense. It is the teacher's responsibility to help students to identify and access existing knowledge, confront and revise misconceptions, and expand and increase knowledge within and across subject areas

(Leinhardt, 1992; Porter & Brophy, 1987, 1988). Anderson and Smith (1987) are among the many researchers who have concluded that the earlier view of teaching as infusing knowledge into a vacuum has been supplanted by the view that teaching involves inducing change in an existing body of knowledge and belief. Reynolds (1992) sums this up as follows: "Competent teachers create lessons that enable students to connect what they know to new information" (p. 10).

McDiarmid (1991) explains that: "Teachers' capacity to evaluate the appropriateness of the representations they make of their subject matter depends, then, on their view of learners as well as on their understanding of the learners' relationship to the subject matter. Representations need to take into account what learners are already likely to know and understand about the subject matter as well as the experiences and knowledge they bring with them from their environment. Representations may be appropriate either because they draw on learners' initial understandings or—if these initial understandings of the subject contravene those of most people in the field—because they force learners to confront their taken-for-granted understandings (Floden, Buchmann, & Schwille, 1987)" (p. 263).

McDiarmid (1991) concludes with three key points that illustrate the importance of this criterion: (a) teachers need to know how school knowledge is perceived in their learners' cultures (a point which also relates to criterion D4, "Communicating with parents or guardians about student learning"); (b) teachers need to know what kind of knowledge, skills, and commitments are valued in the learners' cultures; and (c) teachers need to know about students' prior knowledge of and experience with the subject matter (p. 267).

Related Job Analysis Findings

Wesley et al. (1993) found that this criterion was rated as "moderately important," "very important," or "extremely important" by 88% of those responding and as "very important" or "extremely important" by 58% of those responding. This criterion had a mean rating of 3.55 (on a scale of 0.0 lowest to 5.0 highest) across all respondents. Only three percent of the respondents said that they would not expect this aspect of teaching to have been mastered by the beginning teacher. There was some indication of slightly lower ratings from secondary than from elementary teachers, and from male than from female teachers on this criterion. The ratings for this criterion were lower for science and social studies teachers than for other teachers. This is consistent with findings by Porter and Brophy (1987), which suggest that, in general, teachers of secondary level mathematics and science tend to express less personal responsibility for their students' learning than do other teachers, which would be logically consistent with minimizing the importance of understanding students' background knowledge and experience. In contrast, this criterion was rated higher by special education teachers than by other teachers. More-experienced (six or more years) teachers rated this higher than did less-experienced teachers (0 to five years), and minority teachers rated it higher than did non-minority teachers.

In a prior study, Powers (1992) found ratings of "important" or "very important" from 83% of those responding to the July 1991 version of this criterion ("Become familiar with relevant aspects of students' prior knowledge, skills, experiences, and cultures"). For the spring 1992 sample, 82% of respondents rated the identically worded criterion as "important" or "very important."

Related State Licensing Requirements

States with teacher licensing performance assessment requirements related to this criterion include: Connecticut, Florida, Kentucky, Maine, Mississippi, Missouri, New Mexico, Oklahoma, Tennessee, and Utah (Klem, 1992). Tracy and Smeaton (1993) cite the more global, but closely related, criterion "Instructional planning and preparation" (p. 225), and the closely matched, and more specific, criterion "Addressing individual student differences" (p. 225), as being required by at least two-thirds of the states in their study.

Fieldwork Findings

This criterion was housed in Domain B (as B1) in the summer 1991 version of the criteria (see Appendix E). It was moved to Domain A (Criterion A3) in the January 1992 version of the criteria, on the grounds that the knowledge it focuses on is necessary to any organization or planning that the teacher does prior to actual instruction. In September 1992, the criterion was moved to its current position of primacy, as a prerequisite to all other planning for a given class. In addition, wording was changed from "students' prior knowledge, skills, and cultural resources" to "students' background knowledge and experiences." The description of the criterion was amplified to explain more clearly what the intent of the criterion is, how students' cultural resources fit into it, and what constitutes reasonable expectations for a beginning teacher. In the spring 1992 pilot studies, paired assessors' ratings were within one-half point of each other for 93.2% of the candidates assessed (Livingston, 1993).

Criterion A2: Articulating Clear Learning Goals for the Lesson That Are Appropriate to the Students

CRITERION DESCRIPTION.   A teacher should be able to translate the content of the lesson into goals for student learning. "Goals" should be understood to mean the desired learning outcomes or objectives for the lesson that will be observed. Goals may be expressed in various formats and terminology. It is critical, however, that goals—what the teacher wants the student to learn—be clearly distinguished from activities—what the teacher wants the students to do.

There are no restrictions to the kinds of learning that can be expressed in learning goals. In many cases, goals may refer to knowledge to be acquired—concepts, facts, and so on. In other situations, goals may address other kinds of learning; these may include, but are not limited to, values, thinking skills, social skills, performance skills, and behavioral goals. Regardless of the kind of goals involved, the teacher should be able to articulate how the students' actions, attitudes, knowledge, and/or skills will be modified or enhanced through their participation in the lesson.

At the basic level, this criterion asks teachers to translate their knowledge of content into goals that are stated as general learning outcomes. As the teacher gains skill, he or she should be able to support the goals by explaining why they are appropriate for this particular group of students and to modify or adjust expected outcomes to meet the needs of individual students in the class. If the teacher has no influence over the learning goals set for the class—for example, because of the specific requirements of a district-determined curriculum—the teacher should be able to explain how, and to what extent, the goals are appropriate for the whole class, or for groups or individual students within the class.

Related Research Literature

Jones (1992) concludes from a review of the literature in this area that research in teacher planning has demonstrated that effective teaching and learning are dependent upon the teacher's formulation of learning goals that are appropriate to the students (Brophy & Good, 1986; Walker, 1985). The findings of Clark and Yinger (1977), Peterson, Marx, and Clark (1978), and Stallings and Kaskowitz (1974) support the notion that clear learning goals are directly related to effective teaching and positive classroom behavior, although these goals may be implemented in different ways in different classrooms. Peterson, Marx, and Clark also link the formulation of clear learning goals with teachers' ability to place learning activities in a logical sequence (see Criterion A3, "Demonstrating an understanding of the connections between the content that was learned previously, the current content, and the content that remains to be learned in the future.")

Planning clear and appropriate learning goals permits a sense of confidence and direction for teachers (Clark & Yinger, 1979; McCutcheon, 1980). Porter and Brophy (1987, 1988), in their review of the effective teaching literature, reported that the most effective teachers planned for a variety of academic and social goals for their students. Furthermore, Yinger (1977) and Kauchak and Peterson (1987) suggest that effective teachers engage in a type of long-term planning of learning goals ranging from before the school year begins and continuing through the academic year. Druian and Butler (1987), Hohn (1986), and Natriello (1987) have reported that learning expectations that are too high or too low may keep students from engaging in academic activities.

Related Job Analysis Findings

Wesley et al. (1993) found that this criterion was rated as "moderately important," "very important," or "extremely important" by 98% of those responding and as "very important" or "extremely important" by 87% of those responding. This criterion had a mean rating of 4.28 (on a scale of 0.0 lowest to 5.0 highest) across all respondents. Zero percent of the respondents said that they would not expect this aspect of teaching to have been mastered by the beginning teacher. This criterion did not appear as a separate entry in the July 1991 version of the criteria studied by Powers (1992). For the January 1992 version, Powers found that a similarly worded criterion ("Articulate clear learning goals") was rated as "important" or "very important by" 95% of the respondents.

Related State Licensing Requirements

States with teacher licensing performance assessment requirements related to this criterion include: Connecticut, Florida, Maine, Mississippi, Missouri, New Mexico, Tennessee, and Utah (Klem, 1992). Tracy and Smeaton (1993) cite the closely related, but more global, criterion "Instructional planning and preparation" (p. 225) as being required by at least two-thirds of the states in their study.

Fieldwork Findings

This criterion was added to the January 1992 criteria after the early pilot work indicated that it was needed to help organize the rest of Domain A. In the September 1992 revision, the description was revised to respond to several points of confusion that fieldwork revealed among the assessors: how the term "goals" is defined for the purpose of PRAXIS III assessments; the range of possible goals that may be articulated by the beginning teacher; the distinction between goals and activities; and assessment when the teacher does not control curricular goals. In the spring 1992 pilot studies, paired assessors' ratings were within one-half point of each other for 84.1% of the candidates assessed (Livingston, 1993).

Criterion A3: Demonstrating an Understanding of the Connections Between the Content That Was Learned Previously, the Current Content, and the Content That Remains to Be Learned in the Future

CRITERION DESCRIPTION. This criterion refers to a teacher's understanding of the structure or hierarchy of a discipline and of how knowing one element is prerequisite to or related to learning another. It contains two fundamental ideas. First, the teacher must be able to sequence content across lessons; she or he should be able to explain how the content of the lesson is related to what preceded it and how it is related to what will follow. Second, she or he should be able to draw on knowledge of the subject matter to explain where the current lesson fits within the broader scope of the discipline as a whole. That is, the teacher must be able to explain not only how the content of the lesson fits with what came before and what will follow, but also *why* this sequence is logical.

If the sequencing of content is outside the teacher's control, the teacher should still be able to identify and explain the connections, as well as the relationships, that this criterion addresses.

Related Research Literature

Jones (1992) concludes that research indicates that a logical ordering of the content to be taught enhances student achievement and engagement. Effective teachers understand the content of the lesson in a manner that permits students to relate prior learning to the content, forming a framework for future content (Porter & Brophy, 1987, 1988). Shulman (1987) states, "We expect teachers to understand what they teach and, when possible, to understand it in several ways. They should understand how a given idea relates to other ideas within the same subject area and to ideas in other subjects as well" (p. 14).

Although this criterion is concerned with the knowledge that teachers hold about the subjects they teach, the significance of this knowledge is, in the end, how the teacher's knowledge is transformed to help students learn. Students tend to rate their lesson higher and to be able to increase their achievement levels when they understand how facts, concepts, and principles are interrelated (Smith, 1985; Van Patten, Chao & Reigeluth, 1986). Furthermore, appropriate sequencing and pacing of a lesson permits students to engage in activities that suit their current developmental and achievement levels, interests, and needs (Taylor & Valentine, 1985; Ysseldyke, Christenson & Thurlow, 1987; Zigmond, Sansone, Miller, Donahoe & Kohnke, 1986). Armento (1977) and Smith and Sanders (1981) have shown that students learn better when instruction is logically sequenced. In order to make the logic and organization of their lessons clear to students, teachers must understand the structure of their disciplines themselves. As Shulman (1987) argues, "Comprehended ideas must be transformed in some manner if they are to be taught. To reason one's way through an act of teaching is to think one's way from the subject matter as understood by the teacher into the minds and motivations of learners" (p. 16).

Englemann (1991), working from the point of view of efficiency, points out that: One fact that teachers should know is that the [inappropriate] curriculum sequence is the basic cause of misconceptions. Another fact is that these misconceptions are very costly because reteaching the appropriate concepts or discriminations requires a far greater amount of time than appropriate initial teaching requires (p. 221).

Related Job Analysis Findings

Wesley et al. (1993) found that this criterion was rated as "moderately important," "very important," or "extremely important" by 94% of those responding and as "very important" or "extremely important" by 74% of those responding. This criterion had a mean rating of 3.93 (on a scale of 0.0 lowest to 5.0 highest) across all respondents. Only two percent of the respondents said that they would not expect this aspect of teaching to have been mastered by the beginning teacher.

In an earlier study, Powers (1992) found ratings of "important" or "very important" from 89% of those responding to the July 1991 version of this criterion ("Demonstrate an understanding of the connections between the content that was studied previously, the current content, and the content that remains to be studied in the future"). The identically worded criterion was rated as "important" or "very important" by 88% of the spring 1992 sample.

Related State Licensing Requirements

States with teacher licensing performance assessment requirements related to this criterion include: Connecticut, Florida, Maine, Mississippi, Missouri, Oklahoma, and Tennessee (Klem, 1992). Tracy and Smeaton (1993) cite the more global, but closely related, criterion "Instructional planning and preparation" (p. 225) as being required by at least two-thirds of the states in their study.

Fieldwork Findings

This criterion has been part of the system throughout development, with little change; however, the description and scoring rules underwent a series of revisions. In the September 1992 revision, the description was amplified. The scoring rules were revised, in part to address assessors' opinions that the distinction between levels 2.0 and 3.0 had been unclear. In the spring 1992 pilot studies, paired assessors' ratings were within one-half point of each other for 77.3% of the candidates assessed (Livingston, 1993).

Criterion A4: Creating or Selecting Teaching Methods, Learning Activities, and Instructional Materials or Other Resources That Are Appropriate to the Students and That Are Aligned With the Goals of the Lesson

CRITERION DESCRIPTION. Instructional methods are the various ways in which teachers can structure learning activities. Methods are concerned with what teachers do; activities are concerned with what students do. Learning activities can involve students as a large group, in small groups, or individually. Activities should be designed to foster student involvement and to enhance the learning experience, whether the format is teacher presentation, teacher-led discussion, structured small-group work, peer teaching, programmed instruction, or some other format.

Activities range from teacher-directed through student-initiated. In deciding on teaching methods and selecting or designing learning activities, teachers should consider the learning goals and the preferred participation styles of students in the class. For example, some content is best conveyed through large-group discussion; other content lends itself better to small-group investigation. Similarly, some students may work better individually; others may benefit from cooperative group work. Whether the activities are created by the teacher or selected from those in a textbook or curriculum guide, the teacher should be able to provide a sound rationale for their use.

Instructional materials are concrete resources that students use to learn the content of the lesson. In some situations, no instructional materials are needed. If instructional materials are used, they may support any type of lesson. Materials need not be elaborate or expensive; for example, they may be "found" materials. Teachers should also be able to make use of relevant materials that students bring to class. In addition, the teacher may choose to draw on other resources, such as parents and community institutions. Whatever materials or resources are selected must be appropriate to the students. In a culturally or otherwise diverse classroom, this might require the use of a variety of types of materials.

Methods, activities, materials, and resources must be aligned with each other, and with the goals of the lesson. Activities, materials, and resources must all be developmentally appropriate for the students. At the basic level, this should be true for the students as a group. As teachers gain skill, they should be able to recognize the diverse needs of students and to meet those needs through the use of varied methods, activities, and materials; the teacher's decisions should accommodate students in the class who have specific physical, emotional, behavioral, or learning differences. For a given lesson, teachers should also gain skill at considering the various teaching methods, activities, materials, and resources, and selecting or creating those that will best meet students' needs.

Related Research Literature

Research indicates that effective teachers prepare appropriate instructional materials and plan learning activities that will engage students and assist them in achieving the established learning goals (Clark & Yinger, 1979; Emmer, Sanford, Clements & Martin, 1982; Evertson, Anderson, Anderson & Brophy, 1980; McCutcheon, 1980; Peterson et al., 1978). Shulman (1987) states, "To advance the aims of organized schooling, materials and structures for teaching and learning are created. These include: Curricula with their scopes and sequences; tests and teaching materials..." (p. 9). These materials should be appropriate to the lesson and to the students' abilities and needs (Osborn, Jones, & Stein, 1985; Taylor & Valentine, 1985). Porter and Brophy (1987, 1988) report that effective teachers select materials appropriate to learning goals and individual student characteristics and that such a selection permits more effective use of instructional time as well as an increase in student learning. They state that effective teachers "make expert use of existing instructional materials in order to devote more time to practices that enrich and clarify content" (p. 75). It is during the formulation of plans for a lesson that most teachers consider the appropriate materials and activities (Zahorik, 1975).

Related Job Analysis Findings

Wesley et al. (1993) found that this criterion was rated as "moderately important," "very important," or "extremely important," by 97% of those responding and as "very important" or "extremely important" by 87% of those responding. This criterion had a mean rating of 4.29 (on a scale of 0.0 lowest to 5.0 highest) across all respondents. Only two percent of the respondents said that they would not expect this aspect of teaching to have been mastered by the beginning teacher. In an earlier study, Powers (1992) found ratings of "important" or "very important" from 91% of those responding to the July 1991 version of this criterion ("Create or select appropriate instructional material/other resources and learning activities that are clearly linked to the goals or intents of the lesson"). In the spring 1992 survey, a slightly different version ("Create or select appropriate instructional materials, resources, and learning activities that are appropriate to the students and are clearly linked to the goals and intents of the lesson") was rated as "important" or "very important" by 97% of the sample.

Related State Licensing Requirements

States with teacher licensing performance assessment requirements related to this criterion include: Connecticut, Florida, Kentucky, Maine, Mississippi, Missouri, New Mexico, Oklahoma, and Tennessee (Klem, 1992). Tracy and Smeaton (1993) cite the more global, but closely related, criterion "Instructional planning and preparation" (p. 225) as being required by at least two-thirds of the states in their study. They also cite the closely matched and more specific criterion "Use of instructional materials" (p. 225).

Fieldwork Findings

This criterion has been part of the system throughout development; the notion of explicitly including the idea of appropriateness for students in the class was added for the January 1992 criteria as part of the general revision of Domain A. In the September 1992 revision, teaching methods were specifically included in this criterion. In the spring 1992 pilot studies, paired assessors' ratings were within one-half point of each other for 81.4% of the candidates assessed (Livingston, 1993).

Criterion A5: Creating or Selecting Evaluation Strategies That Are Appropriate for the Students and That Are Aligned With the Goals of the Lesson

CRITERION DESCRIPTION. It is only through well-designed evaluation strategies that a teacher knows whether students have achieved the learning goals for the lesson and is able to plan further learning experiences. Evaluation strategies must be aligned with, and reflect, the goals of the lesson. If the goals relate to *individual* student learning, then the plan for evaluation should do so, too; if the goals relate to *small- or large-group* outcomes, as in a performing music group, then the plan for evaluation should also do so.

A plan for evaluation of student learning may include one or more formats. The teacher may create evaluation strategies (for example, teacher-made tests or student portfolios) or select them from the instructional materials used (for example, the chapter test from a textbook). For certain types of goals, tests may be less appropriate than other strategies, such as observation of student performance. Many teachers involve students in self-evaluation or peer evaluation. Whatever the strategy, evaluation must be systematic. That is, it must provide the teacher with useful information about the extent to which the instructional goals—whether individual or group—have been met. As the teacher gains experience, she or he will gain understanding of how the results of the evaluation can be used to help in planning future instruction.

Evaluation strategies must be appropriate for the students. Since the goal of evaluation is to gather information about learning, the strategies chosen should provide students with clear opportunities to demonstrate their learning. In culturally diverse classrooms, student evaluation is especially complex. Children from different groups may enter school with culturally specific understandings of the appropriate ways of displaying knowledge. If the teacher and students do not share these understandings, the teacher may misjudge the students' competence unless he or she is sensitive to these cultural differences. Because reliance on a single form of evaluation may place some students at a disadvantage, teachers may need to use a variety of strategies to evaluate student learning. This is especially relevant for students of limited English proficiency and for many students with exceptionalities.

Evaluation strategies may be implemented at a time later than the observed lesson. While some monitoring of student learning occurs in class on a daily basis, most systematic evaluation is separated in time from instruction. The nature of the lesson and the unit will determine not only the form but also the timing of evaluation. In many cases, evaluation of the lesson being assessed may be part of the evaluation of a longer unit of instruction.

A critical element of this criterion is that the strategy or plan is designed to provide information about how well the learning goals of this lesson have been met. In most cases, the assessor will *not* see the evaluation strategies being implemented; however, the teacher must provide oral or written evidence of a plan for the evaluation of learning goals.

Related Research Literature

Effective teachers plan for the evaluation of student progress in relationship to the stated learning goals. Effective teachers are consistent in evaluating students' progress and design the evaluations so that they can be used for feedback to students (Brophy & Good, 1986; Porter & Brophy, 1987, 1988; Reynolds, 1992; Rosenshine, 1987; Zigmond et al. (1986). Peterson, et al. (1978) also suggest that planning appropriate evaluation strategies can foster effective teaching and learning. In addition, research in evaluation suggests that multiple forms of evidence provide a more accurate picture of student progress than does any single instrument. Performance assessments, interviews, and questionnaires are some of the supplements to standardized tests (Cryan, 1986).

The American Federation of Teachers, the National Council for Measurement in Education, and the National Education Association (1992) have developed seven research-based standards for teachers' evaluation of students. These standards relate to choosing assessment methods, developing them, administering them, using the results of assessments, using evaluation information as part of pupil grading, communicating assessment results, and using assessments ethically.

Merwin (1989) concludes a review of the literature in this area as follows: "A teacher will be effective to the extent that he or she knows how to evaluate student characteristics and program characteristics and understands the relationships among them" (p. 191).

Related Job Analysis Findings

Wesley et al. (1993) found that this criterion was rated as "moderately important," "very important," or "extremely important" by 96% of those responding and as "very important" or "extremely important" by 80% of those responding. This criterion had a mean rating of 4.06 (on a scale of 0.0 lowest to 5.0 highest) across all respondents. Only two percent of the respondents said that they would not expect this aspect of teaching to have been mastered by the beginning teacher. In an earlier study, Powers (1992) found ratings of "important" or "very important" from 90% of those responding to the July 1991 version of this criterion ("Create or select appropriate evaluation strategies that are clearly linked to the goals or intents of the lesson"). In the spring 1992 survey, a slightly different version ("Create or select evaluation strategies that are appropriate to the students and are linked to the intents or goals of the lesson") was rated as "important" or "very important" by 95% of the sample.

Related State Licensing Requirements

States with teacher licensing performance assessment requirements related to this criterion include: Connecticut, Florida, Mississippi, Missouri, and Oklahoma (Klem, 1992). Tracy and Smeaton (1993) cite the more global but closely related criterion "Instructional planning and preparation" (p. 225) as being required by at least two-thirds of the states in their study. They also cite the closely matched and more specific criterion "Evaluation of student progress" (p. 225).

Fieldwork Findings

This criterion was originally part of what is now Criterion A4 ("Creating or selecting teaching methods, learning activities, and instructional materials or other resources that are appropriate for the students and that are aligned with the goals of the lesson"); it became independent in the summer of 1991. The explicit idea of appropriateness for students was added for the January 1992 criteria, as part of the general revision of Domain A. The scoring rules for this criterion have been among the most stable; in the September 1992 revision, the description was amplified. In the spring 1992 pilot studies, paired assessors' ratings were within one-half point of each other for 86.0% of the candidates assessed (Livingston, 1993).

Domain B: Creating an Environment for Student Learning

Domain B relates to the social and emotional components of learning as prerequisites to academic achievement. Thus, most of the criteria in this domain focus on the human interactions in the classroom, on the connections between teachers and students, and among students. Domain B addresses issues of fairness and rapport, of helping students to believe that they can learn and can meet challenges, of establishing and maintaining constructive standards for behavior in the classroom. It also includes the learning "environment" in the most literal sense—the physical setting in which teaching and learning take place.

A learning environment that provides both emotional and physical safety for students is one in which a broad range of teaching and learning experiences can occur. Teachers must be able to use their knowledge of their students in order to interpret their students' behavior accurately and respond in ways that are appropriate and supportive. When they do so, their interactions with students consistently foster the students' sense of self-esteem. In addition, teachers' efforts to establish a sense of the classroom as a community with clear standards should never be arbitrary; all behavioral standards and teacher-student interactions should be grounded in a sense of respect for students as individuals.

Domain B consists of the following five criteria.

Criterion B1: Creating a Climate That Promotes Fairness

CRITERION DESCRIPTION. This criterion is concerned with the teacher's ability to facilitate and maintain fair classroom interactions between the teacher and the students and among students. "Fairness" here means helping all students to have access to learning and to feel that they are equally valued in the classroom. In this sense, promoting fairness also implies promoting a sense of self-worth for each student. The teacher should consistently provide good examples of fairness. At the same time, fair treatment should *not* be interpreted to mean a formulaic, rigid, or stereotype-based way of "treating all students the same."

The teacher must be fair in the treatment of students of different genders, ethnicity, cultural backgrounds, and socioeconomic levels, as well as those with exceptionalities. The teacher should be familiar with and value the diverse ways in which students express themselves and interact with one another. Examples of unfair teacher behavior include giving praise to high achievers only, "playing favorites," allowing particular individuals or groups of students to be consistently off-task without trying to reengage them in the activity, asking or allowing only some students to respond to questions, making comments about students that are demeaning, and stereotyping. In contrast, to create a climate that promotes fairness, the teacher should convey and act on the attitude that all students are important and that they all have a right to learning opportunities and attention. The teacher should not accept without a response comments and interactions by students with each other or with the teacher that are demeaning, based on stereotypes, or otherwise unfair.

As the teacher gains skill, she or he should be able to help students develop a sense of fairness—what it means and how it takes shape—in their interactions with each other.

Related Research Literature

Effective teachers manage their classrooms so as to create a climate that fosters fair and equitable interactions (Brophy, 1987; Doyle, 1986; Paine, 1989). Brophy (1987) reports that "Consistent *projection of positive expectations, attributions, and social labels* to the students is important in fostering positive self-concepts and related motives that orient them toward pro-social behavior. In short, students who are consistently treated as if they are well-intentioned individuals who respect themselves and others and desire to act responsibly, morally, and pro-socially are more likely to live up to these expectations and acquire these qualities than students who are treated as if they had the opposite qualities. This is all the more likely if their positive qualities and behaviors are *reinforced,* not so much through material rewards as through expressions of appreciation delivered in ways likely to increase the students' tendencies to attribute their desirable behavior to their own desirable underlying personal traits and to reinforce themselves for possessing and acting on the basis of these traits..." (p. 23-24).

Good (1990) reviews the work he has done with Brophy and others (e.g., Cooper & Good, 1983; Good & Brophy, 1986) that details the importance of fairness in the classroom, particularly in its effect on student thinking. Teacher practices related to lack of development of student thinking skills include: criticizing low achievers more frequently than others and criticizing high achievers for incorrect responses; praising low achievers less than others for correct responses; praising marginal or incorrect answers given by low achievers, but not by high achievers. This research is also pertinent to criterion B3, "Communicating challenging learning expectations to each student."

Grant (1991) summarizes numerous studies relating fairness concerns to both student achievement and educational policy. McDiarmid (1991) also gives an overview and theoretical analysis of the links between fairness, individualization, and learning.

Villegas (1991, 1992) also summarizes the literature related to creating a classroom climate that promotes fairness, and concludes that equitable behavior of teachers and students is a major contributor to improving the classroom climate and positively affecting student learning.

Related Job Analysis Findings

Wesley et al. (1993) found that this criterion was rated as "moderately important," "very important," or "extremely important" by 99% of those responding and as "very important" or "extremely important" by 89% of those responding. This criterion had a mean rating of 4.47 (on a scale of 0.0 lowest to 5.0 highest) across all respondents. Zero percent of the respondents said that they would not expect this aspect of teaching to have been mastered by the beginning teacher. In an earlier study, Powers (1992) found ratings of "important" or "very important" from 98% of both samples of those responding to earlier versions of this criterion ("Create a classroom climate that ensures equity and respect for and among students, and between students and the teacher" [July 1991 version]; and "Create a climate that ensures equity among students and between teachers and students" [January 1992 version]).

Related State Licensing Requirements

States with teacher licensing performance assessment requirements related to this criterion include: Connecticut, Florida, Kentucky, Maine, Mississippi, Missouri, New Mexico, North Carolina, Oklahoma, Tennessee, and Utah (Klem, 1992). Tracy and Smeaton (1993) cite the more global but closely related criterion "Maintenance of classroom climate conducive to learning" (p. 225) as being required by at least two-thirds of the states in their study.

Fieldwork Findings

In September 1992, the order of Domains B and C was switched. In the September revision, a wording change was made from "equity" to "fairness." In the 1991-1992 pilot studies, the interrelated ideas of fairness, promoting students' self-worth, and promoting or modeling respectful interactions that were present in what are now criteria B1, B2, and B3 had caused the assessors some uncertainty about the correct placement of evidence from the interviews and observations. In the September 1992 revision, therefore, we attempted to clarify those distinctions. In the spring 1992 pilot studies, paired assessors' ratings were within one-half point of each other for 81.8% of the candidates assessed (Livingston, 1993).

Criterion B2: Establishing and Maintaining Rapport With Students

CRITERION DESCRIPTION.   This criterion is concerned with the teacher's ability to relate positively to students as people. The teacher might demonstrate traits such as genuine concern, warmth, sincerity, and humor. Additional ways of establishing rapport include exhibiting interest in students as unique individuals, acknowledging the traditions and customs of students with differing ethnic backgrounds, and taking time to listen to students. Effective interpersonal and communication skills also contribute to establishing rapport. Comments that indicate, either directly or indirectly, an understanding of students' lives outside of school also provide evidence of rapport. Other indicators of rapport can include making eye contact, smiling, making focused comments or a friendly joke, maintaining appropriate proximity to students, and so on.

Rapport can appear in a wide range of forms. Students' developmental levels will have a significant impact on what constitutes appropriate attempts to establish rapport. For example, some kinds of physical contact may be appropriate with young children, but inappropriate with older students. In addition, teachers, like students, are diverse; there is no single "right way" to achieve rapport. Because teacher-student rapport can be manifested in so many different ways, the assessor must be careful to consider rapport in specific rather than general terms; is the teacher's attempt to establish or maintain rapport appropriate, given the context in which the teacher is working? For example, a comment by a teacher might be interpreted as undesirably sarcastic in one context, but as supportive in another. In such a situation, the assessor must consider the students' reactions, or ask about the interaction in the post-observation interview.

As the teacher gains skill, he or she should be able to build on a basis of understanding students and should have a better sense of what is appropriate and likely to work with students.

Related Research Literature

The work of Keith, Tormatzky, and Pettigrew (1974), Rosenshine (1971), and Walberg, Schiller, and Haertel (1979) supports the notion that teacher enthusiasm and a positive climate in the classroom are correlated with high student achievement. Positive morale and interest in the subject matter also appear to be related to the establishment of a rapport with students, which leads to supportive relationships between teachers and students (Fraser, 1986; Haertel, Walberg, & Haertel, 1981; Moors, 1979). Leinhardt (1992) also addresses the cultural and social dimensions of knowledge—it is produced, shared, transformed, and distributed among members of a community. The teacher, as a member of this classroom community, functions as a highly knowledgeable guide whose role it is to facilitate the acquisition and expand the amount of information available within this group.

Brophy (1987) has proposed some strategies to establish appropriate rapport with a variety of students. He summarizes a variety of strategies for establishing rapport to facilitate learning and concludes that "These are basic socialization skills that most if not all teachers are likely to need and use frequently…" (p. 25). In addition, in order to establish appropriate rapport with students, teachers need to be aware of culturally based differences in social interactions that may result in misinterpretations of social as well as academic behaviors (Hilliard, 1989; Irvine, 1989; Kochman, 1981; Villegas, 1991).

Related Job Analysis Findings

Wesley et al. (1993) found that this criterion was rated as "moderately important," "very important," or "extremely important" by 97% of those responding and as "very important" or "extremely important" by 84% of those responding. This criterion had a mean rating of 4.22 (on a scale of 0.0 lowest to 5.0 highest) across all respondents. Only one percent of the respondents said that they would not expect this aspect of teaching to have been mastered by the beginning teacher. In an earlier study, Powers (1992) found ratings of "important" or "very important" from 92% of those responding to the July 1991 version of this criterion ("Establish and maintain rapport with students in ways that are appropriate to the students' developmental needs"). In the spring 1992 survey, the identically worded criterion was rated as "important" or "very important" by 89% of the sample.

Related State Licensing Requirements

States with teacher licensing performance assessment requirements related to this criterion include: Connecticut, Florida, Mississippi, Missouri, New Mexico, Oklahoma, and Utah (Klem, 1992). Tracy and Smeaton (1993) cite the more global, but closely related, criterion "Maintenance of classroom climate conducive to learning" (p. 225) as being required by at least two-thirds of the states in their study.

Fieldwork Findings

This criterion has been part of the system throughout development. Revisions of the description have focused on clarifying what rapport is and what constitutes evidence of it, as well as on trying to convey the wide range of guises rapport can take with different students and different teachers. In the spring 1992 pilot studies, paired assessors' ratings were within one-half point of each other for 83.3% of the candidates assessed (Livingston, 1993).

Criterion B3: Communicating Challenging Learning Expectations to Each Student

CRITERION DESCRIPTION. The teacher must convey the attitude that school is a place for learning and that *all* students can learn. The teacher should communicate explicitly or implicitly a belief that each student is capable of significant achievement. For example, the teacher might select learning goals that are rigorous or challenging for the students, but within their reach, and combine this with encouragement for students to have confidence, to take risks, and in general to strive for success.

Given the likelihood that students in the class will have varying levels of skills, abilities, and achievements, the challenging expectations for each student may—in absolute terms—be somewhat different. A reciprocal relationship frequently exists between expectations and performance. Other things being equal, students may put forth more effort, with greater energy, if they believe that their teacher anticipates that they will perform well. As a result of this effort and energy, students' work frequently meets a high standard, enhancing the students' capabilities in the eyes of the teacher, and encouraging the teacher to hold high standards for future work.

This criterion includes two distinct, though related, ideas. First, a teacher's confidence in students can help them "stretch," tackling challenging tasks or understanding difficult concepts. Second, a teacher's high standards for students can encourage them to produce work of high quality, completed with conscientious attention, that becomes a source of pride for the students. As the teacher gains skill, he or she should be able to draw on familiarity with students' background knowledge and experiences to communicate challenging expectations that are suitable for individual students or groups of students.

Related Research Literature

Research on expectations has concluded that student achievement increases when teachers clearly communicate high expectations to students. In increasingly culturally and ethnically diverse classroom settings, teachers' judgments regarding the academic potential of individual students has a documented effect on students' academic behavior (Irvine, 1990; Rist, 1970; Rosenthal, 1973). The U.S. Department of Education report, *What Works* (1987) found that among the most important characteristics of effective schools is high teacher expectations for student achievement. Stallings's (1982) review of effective strategies for teaching low-achieving secondary school pupils found that effective classroom teachers maintain high expectations for their students. In addition, Rutter, Maugham, Mortimore, Ouston, and Smith's 1979 study of 12 London inner-city schools reported that higher teacher expectations correlated positively with higher achievement. Holliday (1985) reported that Black children's academic achievement was more significantly affected by the teacher's perception of their ability than by their own self-perception. Furthermore, Baker (1973) and Krupczak (1972) have reported that, in general, minority students are more negatively affected by teachers' lowered expectations than are non-minority students.

Jones (1992) notes that high expectations are also reflected in the curriculum. Irvine (1990), Levin (1987), Moll (1988), Oakes (1986), and Stage (1989) argue that the lower academic performance of some minority students is, in part, a result of a "watered-down" curriculum that precludes the development of higher-order thinking. They therefore urge teachers of ethnically and linguistically diverse students to be certain to provide instruction that encourages students to extend their thinking (see also Criterion C3, "Encouraging students to extend their thinking"). Irvine (1990) argues that "how minority children feel about themselves is to a large extent determined by how the child perceives the teacher feels about him or her" (p.19). High and appropriate teacher expectations are an important component of both the effective schools and effective teaching research.

Related Job Analysis Findings

Wesley et al. (1993) found that this criterion was rated as "moderately important," "very important," or "extremely important" by 95% of those responding and as "very important" or "extremely important" by 74% of those responding. This criterion had a mean rating of 3.95 (on a scale of 0.0 lowest to 5.0 highest) across all respondents. Only three percent of the respondents said that they would not expect this aspect of teaching to have been mastered by the beginning teacher. In an earlier study, Powers (1992) found ratings of "important" or "very important" from 95% of those responding to the July 1991 version of this criterion ("Set high expectations for each student, make learning expectations clear to students, and help students accept responsibility for their own learning"). In the spring 1992 survey, two similarly worded criteria were rated: One ("Making learning expectations clear to students") was rated as "important" or "very important" by 96% of the sample. The other ("Communicate high expectations for each student") was rated as "important" or "very important" by 92% of the sample.

Related State Licensing Requirements

States with teacher licensing performance assessment requirements related to this criterion include: Connecticut, Mississippi, and Missouri (Klem, 1992). Tracy and Smeaton (1993) cite the more global, but closely related, criterion "Maintenance of classroom climate conducive to learning" (p. 225) as being required by at least two-thirds of the states in their study.

Fieldwork Findings

In the January 1992 criteria, this criterion was the first in what was labelled Domain B at that time (Teaching for Student Learning), with slightly different wording. Pilot results showed that assessors experienced some difficulty in discerning what constituted evidence for it, and some confusion as to its precise intent. This criterion was moved to the current Domain B for the September 1992 version on the grounds that what is intended here is more logically part of the learning environment and the psychological aspects of the classroom. In addition, the description was extensively revised and amplified, and the scoring rules were rewritten. In the spring

1992 pilot studies, paired assessors' ratings were within one-half point of each other for 76.7% of the candidates assessed (Livingston, 1993).

Criterion B4: Establishing and Maintaining Consistent Standards of Classroom Behavior

CRITERION DESCRIPTION. This criterion refers to the desired standards of teacher and student interaction that will ensure an appropriate climate for learning. Both students and teacher may contribute to the development of standards for appropriate classroom behavior. The exact nature of such standards may vary widely, in response to students' developmental levels, their cultural backgrounds, the subject being taught, the model of teaching that is implemented, the level of noise or informality that the teacher is comfortable with, and so on. Once established and agreed on, these standards must be maintained consistently, although there will, of course, be situations that require "exceptions to the rule."

It is not expected that all students will behave at all times in accordance with the behavioral standards for the class. Students as individuals obviously differ widely in their attitudes and their willingness to accept behavioral standards; in addition, classes, as groups, have their own "personalities." In all cases, it is important for the teacher both to demonstrate positive behavior and to make sure that students understand the consequences for breaches of the agreed-on standards of behavior. At the basic level, teachers may have trouble anticipating potentially disruptive behavior and may, therefore, have to respond frequently to major disruptions (that is, behavior that constitutes a serious breach of the standards for the class). As the teacher gains skill she or he should be able to move to a level of skill that enables her or him to handle the range of behavior issues more consistently and effectively and to anticipate misbehavior.

The assessor should not expect to see the teacher actively establishing standards for behavior during every lesson that is observed; in many cases, the students' behavior may enable the assessor to infer that standards have been established and maintained. In evaluating how standards of behavior have been established, implemented, and maintained, it is also important to keep in mind that there is a range of standards for behavior that can contribute to a range of positive learning environments. There is no single right way to keep order. In all cases, however, the standards must embody a sense of respect for students as people.

If there are school policies that affect standards of classroom behavior, the assessor should be aware of them and of the rationale for them.

Related Research Literature

Research on classroom management points to the importance of maintaining consistent standards of behavior for students in regular education and special education settings (Brophy, 1987; Brophy & Good, 1986; Gage, 1978; Stallings, 1982; U.S. Department of Education, 1987; Zigmond et al. (1986).

Herman and Tramontana (1971) showed that establishing clear guidelines for student behavior leads to less disruptive behavior in the classroom and increased student learning. The work of Emmer, Evertson, and Anderson (1980), Emmer (1982) and Evertson, Emmer, Sanford, and Clements (1983) suggests that effective classroom management involves frequent and explicit direction to students regarding expected standards of behavioral conduct. Emmer et al. (1980), who observed elementary classrooms at the beginning of the school year, found that in better-managed elementary level classrooms, "As soon as most students had arrived the teachers began describing rules and procedures... The rules and procedures were explained clearly, with examples and reasons. Not all procedures were discussed, only those that were needed for initial activities" (p. 7). In addition, Doyle (1986) reported that, "Obviously the tasks of promoting learning and order are closely intertwined: Some minimal level of orderliness is necessary for instruction to occur and lessons must be sufficiently well constructed to capture and sustain student attention. Indeed, the tasks exist simultaneously so that a teacher often faces competing pressures to maximize learning and sustain order" (p. 395). He further concluded that "Effective managers, however, integrated their rules and procedures into a workable system and deliberately taught this system to the students. Rules and procedures were concrete, explicit, and functional, that is, they contributed to order and work accomplishment. In addition, items were clearly explained to students, signals were used to indicate when actions were to be carried out or stopped, and time was spent rehearsing procedures" (p. 410). Evertson and Harris (1992) emphasize the need to establish routines and procedures, and teach them along with expectations for appropriate performance.

Brophy (1987) also emphasized the importance of establishing sets of classroom routines: "*Routines* are standardized methods of handling particular situations. Many of these are consciously adopted by the teacher and even taught to the students in the form of classroom rules and procedures. By banning certain activities and requiring that other activities be done at certain times or in certain ways, rules and procedures simplify the complexities of life in classrooms for both teachers and students by imposing structures that make events more predictable. This reduces the students' needs to seek direction and the teacher's need to make decisions or give specific instructions concerning everyday events" (p. 6-7).

Related Job Analysis Findings

Wesley et al. (1993) found that this criterion was rated as "moderately important," "very important," or "extremely important" by 98% of those responding and as "very important" or "extremely important" by 94% of those responding. This criterion had a mean rating of 4.58 (on a scale of 0.0 lowest to 5.0 highest), the highest in the survey, across all respondents. Only one percent of the respondents said that they would not expect this aspect of teaching to have been mastered by the beginning teacher. In an earlier study, Powers (1992) found ratings of "important" or "very important" from 97% of those responding to the July 1991 version of this criterion ("Establish and consistently maintain clear standards of behavior in order to ensure an appropriate climate for learning"). In the spring 1992 survey, a similarly worded criterion ("Establish and maintain consistent, respectful standards of classroom interaction and behavior") was rated "important" or "very important" by 97% of the respondents.

Related State Licensing Requirements

States with teacher licensing performance assessment requirements related to this criterion include: Connecticut, Florida, Kentucky, Mississippi,

Missouri, New Mexico, North Carolina, Oklahoma, Tennessee, and Utah (Klem, 1992). Tracy and Smeaton (1993) cite the more global, but closely related, criterion "Maintenance of classroom climate conducive to learning" (p. 225) as being required by at least two-thirds of the states in their study.

Fieldwork Findings

This criterion has been part of the system throughout the development of PRAXIS III. Revision from January 1992 to September 1992 focused on clarifying the content and the limits of the criterion, particularly in relation to the content of Criteria B1 and B2. In addition, this criterion's description was revised for September 1992 to emphasize the range of possibilities for establishing and maintaining consistent standards, and some of the ways in which they may diverge in different classroom contexts. In the spring 1992 pilot studies, paired assessors' ratings were within one-half point of each other for 84.1% of the candidates assessed (Livingston, 1993).

Criterion B5: Making the Physical Environment as Safe and Conducive to Learning as Possible

CRITERION DESCRIPTION. This criterion focuses on the physical setting in which learning is to take place—the degree of harmony or match between the arrangement of the physical environment and the planned lesson or activity. Student safety and students' diverse physical needs also fall within the realm of this criterion.

In assessing this criterion, it is essential to consider the degree of control that the teacher has over the physical environment. For example, if the furniture is securely anchored to the floor or if the teacher moves from classroom to classroom, serious limitations are placed on the teacher's opportunities to demonstrate effective use of space.

When the teacher does have control of the learning space, the assessor's attention should focus on the effect that the physical arrangements have on learning. In some situations, such as lab sciences, vocational education, or home economics, it is especially important for the arrangement to reflect a concern for students' safety. In addition, the room should be organized so that all students, including those with special needs, have access to instruction. If the teacher has no control over the physical environment, attention should be given to how the teacher adjusts the lesson or activity to the setting, despite this drawback. As the teacher gains skill, he or she is able to use the physical space as a resource that facilitates learning—that is, the physical space becomes an element that contributes to the effectiveness of instruction. For example, a French or ESL teacher might label the door, windows, shelves, and other objects in the classroom in the language being taught. In a primary-grade classroom, the teacher might take care to position bulletin-board displays and other visual materials at the children's eye level.

Another factor to consider in this criterion is the affective dimension of the physical setting. The presence or absence of displays of student work, the level of diversity evident in displays, the attractiveness of the space, and the degree of overall appeal as a place for learning are variables in this aspect of the criterion. Though such characteristics may be highly variable according to context and relatively difficult to judge, they are part of the decision concerning "conducive to learning" included here.

Related Research Literature

Effective teachers use the physical space of the classroom to facilitate and enhance student learning. Evertson (1989) provides a comprehensive overview of the research supporting the importance of physical factors on student learning and minimizing student misbehavior. Specific studies address such factors as effect on student participation rates, student teacher contacts, time on task, attention, and engagement (e.g., Adams & Biddle, 1970; Anderson, Evertson & Emmer, 1979; Brophy, 1983; Doyle, 1986; Emmer, Evertson, Sanford, Clements, & Worsham 1989. Good and Brophy (1984, 1986) report a positive relationship between student engagement in learning and a well-arranged learning environment. Doyle (1986) reports that: "From the perspective of order, one can easily imagine how furniture arrangements (e.g., circles, U-shapes, straight rows), types of desks and chairs (e.g., tables or booths in art and laboratory rooms vs. conventional desks), and room dividers (e.g., bookcases, file cabinets) could affect the density of students, opportunities for interaction, and the visibility of behavior. Similarly, glare from overhead projectors or light through a window could well create blind spots for a teacher and thus interfere with monitoring classroom behavior" (p. 402).

Goss and Ingersoll (1981) have shown that well-arranged classrooms contribute positively to student engagement with learning tasks. Morine-Dershimer (1977) has shown that teachers who specifically attend to the physical characteristics of their classrooms have students with higher achievement levels than teachers who do not attend to this aspect of classroom life.

Related Job Analysis Findings

Wesley et al. (1993) found that this criterion was rated as "moderately important," "very important," or "extremely important" by 99% of those responding and as "very important" or "extremely important" by 91% of those responding. This criterion had a mean rating of 4.45 (on a scale of 0.0 lowest to 5.0 highest) across all respondents. Zero percent of the respondents said that they would not expect this aspect of teaching to have been mastered by the beginning teacher. In an earlier study, Powers (1992) found ratings of "important" or "very important" from 84% of those responding to the July 1991 version of this criterion ("Make the physical environment as conducive to learning as possible"). In the spring 1992 survey, the identically worded criterion was rated "important" or "very important" by 75% of the respondents.

Related State Licensing Requirements

States with teacher licensing performance assessment requirements related to this criterion include: Connecticut, Florida, Maine, Missouri, Oklahoma, Tennessee, and Utah (Klem, 1992). Tracy and Smeaton (1993) cite the more global, but closely related, criterion "Maintenance of classroom climate conducive to learning" (p. 225) as being required by at least two-thirds of the states in their study.

Fieldwork Findings

This criterion has been part of the system throughout development. In the September 1992 revision, the description and scoring rules were revised to accommodate circumstances in which the teacher's control over the physical environment is severely limited. In the spring 1992 pilot studies, paired assessors' ratings were within one-half point of each other for 86.4% of the candidates assessed (Livingston, 1993).

Domain C: Teaching for Student Learning

This domain focuses on the act of teaching and its overall goal: helping students to connect with the content. As used here, "content" refers to the subject matter of a discipline and may include knowledge, skills, perceptions, and values in any domain: cognitive, social, artistic, physical and so on. Teachers direct students in the process of establishing individual connections with the content, thereby devising a good "fit" for the content within the framework of the students' knowledge, interests, abilities, cultural backgrounds, and personal backgrounds. At the same time, teachers should help students to move beyond the limits of their current knowledge or understanding. Teachers monitor learning, making certain that students assimilate information accurately and that they understand and can apply what they have learned. Teachers must also be sure that students understand what is expected of them procedurally during the lesson and that class time is used to good purpose.

Domain C consists of the following five criteria.

Criterion C1: Making Learning Goals and Instructional Procedures Clear to Students

CRITERION DESCRIPTION. This criterion relates to clear communication of both the learning goals for the specific lesson and the instructional procedures that will be used to attain these goals. There are many ways of communicating learning goals to the students. Sometimes the teacher will make the learning goals explicit for the students at the beginning of the lesson, either orally or in writing. This explicit approach is usually used in direct instruction. At other times, the teacher will wait until the end of the lesson, then help the students to infer the learning goals. This implicit approach is often used in inquiry or discovery lessons. Regardless of the instructional strategy used by the teacher, whether direct or indirect, the students should understand that instruction is purposeful.

Students also need to understand the instructional procedures for the lesson—that is, how they are expected to participate in learning activities. Teachers can communicate instructional procedures in a variety of ways that may include, but are not limited to, oral or written directions, explanations or review of the tasks at hand, written contracts with individual students. All instructions or directions given to students about learning activities should be clear, regardless of the specific focus—e.g., completing a worksheet, performing a complex experiment, creating a work of art, cooperating in a group project. In addition, if an out-of-class assignment is given to students, the procedures for carrying out the assignment should be clear.

As the teacher gains experience, he or she should communicate to students, either implicitly or explicitly, how the instructional procedures for the lesson are related to the learning goals.

Related Research Literature

Effective teachers communicate clearly about goals, learning expectations, and specific instructions for meeting these goals and expectations. Edmonds and Frederickson (1978) report that effective schools serving poor children were characterized by leaders who set clear goals and learning objectives. Brophy & Good (1986) provide a research-based rationale for students' being helped by the teacher to understand the learning expectations of the class and how to get help to achieve those goals. Brophy and Putnam (1979) reviewed the research literature in this area and concluded that teachers' providing clear directions about procedures is linked to student accountability and conduct.

Rosenshine (1987) has shown the importance of clarity in written communications with students.

Research by Delpit (1988) links the concept of clarity in this area to concern about fairness. For students for whom there exists a discrepancy between home and school ways of thinking, questioning, and valuing, it is particularly important for teachers to provide explicit articulation of learning expectations. Delpit suggests that "...students must be *taught* the codes needed to participate fully in the mainstream of American life, not by being forced to attend to hollow, inane, decontextualized subskills, but rather within the context of meaningful communicative endeavors; that they must be allowed the resource of the teacher's expert knowledge while being helped to acknowledge their own 'expertness' as well..." (p. 296).

Related Job Analysis Findings

Wesley et al. (1993) found that this criterion was rated as "moderately important," "very important," or "extremely important" by 97% of those responding and as "very important" or "extremely important" by 85% of those responding. This criterion had a mean rating of 4.25 (on a scale of 0.0 lowest to 5.0 highest) across all respondents. Only one percent of the respondents said that they would not expect this aspect of teaching to have been mastered by the beginning teacher. In an earlier study, Powers (1992) found ratings of "important" or "very important" from 93% of those responding to the July 1991 version of this criterion ("Make content comprehensible to students"). In the spring 1992 survey, the identically worded criterion was rated "important" or "very important" by 99% of the respondents.

Related State Licensing Requirements

States with teacher licensing performance assessment requirements related to this criterion include: Connecticut, Florida, Maine, Mississippi, Tennessee, and Utah (Klein, 1992).

Fieldwork Findings

In the January 1992 criteria, this criterion was stated as "Making learning expectations clear to students." The pilot studies indicated some confusion among assessors about the difference between making goals and procedures clear, and holding high expectations for student learning. The criterion was revised and its description clarified in the September 1992 revision as "Making learning goals and instructional procedures clear to students" (the concept of high expectations for student learning is now in Criterion B3, "Communicating challenging learning expectations to each student"). The description of this criterion focuses on the range of ways in which learning goals can be communicated and on defining instructional procedures. In the spring 1992 pilot studies, paired assessors' ratings were within one-half point of each other for 79.1% of the candidates assessed (Livingston, 1993).

Criterion C2: Making Content Comprehensible to Students

CRITERION DESCRIPTION. This criterion focuses on how the teacher's understanding and organization of content—central issues of Domain A—come to life in the classroom. When the teacher is able to make an effective transition from thinking about content to involving students with it, the content is comprehensible to students; that is, students are able to learn by connecting the new content being taught with what is already familiar to them.

In order to learn, students must be engaged with the content, and the content must be meaningful to them on some level, whether that level is deeply personal or more purely academic. Therefore, one aspect of this criterion is the teacher's skill at activating and building on students' background knowledge and experiences in order to make the content meaningful to them. The content being taught and the particular situation will, of course, influence how the teacher goes about this. For example, reviews of the content may help students to activate relevant knowledge. Questions or discussions that draw on students' experiences outside of school may enable them to draw on less-academic knowledge that will help them to become engaged with and understand the content of the lesson. Such strategies provide opportunities to help students of diverse backgrounds or needs make connections with the content and become engaged with learning. Because student engagement is not likely to occur if the content is incomprehensible, engagement can, in many situations, serve as sound evidence that the students understand the content. However, it is essential to recognize that engagement should involve genuine processing of content, not merely looking busy or becoming involved in activities that are irrelevant to the learning goals.

The teacher should be able to organize instruction through a variety of approaches, such as presentations, small-group or individual work, and student-initiated projects. Such approaches may be used in direct instruction by the teacher or be incorporated into lessons in which students have more control over the learning environment. When the teacher is communicating content directly, it must be clear and accurate, and the teacher should use his or her content knowledge in developing explanations, descriptions, examples, analogies, metaphors, demonstrations, discussions, and learning activities that build bridges to the students' background knowledge and experience. If the teacher uses a relatively nondirective approach (e.g., an inquiry lesson) that allows the students more control over the learning experience, the process or structure of the lesson should itself contribute to making content comprehensible.

Related Research Literature

The essence of teaching is making the content comprehensible to students. Shulman (1987) states that "...the key to distinguishing the knowledge base of teaching lies at the intersection of content and pedagogy, in the capacity of a teacher to transform the content knowledge he or she possesses into forms that are pedagogically powerful and yet adaptive to the variations in ability and background presented by the students" (p. 15). As noted above in the discussion of research literature related to criterion A1 ("Becoming familiar with relevant aspects of students' background knowledge and experiences"), this transformation requires adaptation and tailoring to the individual student (Shulman, 1987), and has roots in the psychological study of schema theory (Glaser, 1984; Floden, 1991).

As also noted above, Villegas (1992) and others conclude that teachers can help students from a wide variety of cultural backgrounds to profit from classroom culture by building on students' cultural resources (p. 7). This entails extending the core concept of knowing about and building on students' prior knowledge, the essence of good teaching, to students of all cultural backgrounds. This essentially constructivist orientation links the knowledge of the student's existing concepts to the interactive process of teaching and learning.

Reynolds (1992) and many others have defined techniques that effective teachers employ in making content comprehensible in a variety of teaching contexts. Rosenshine & Stevens (1986) found that in presenting new material it is most effective to "...proceed in small steps and provide practice on one step before adding another. In this way, the learner does not have to process too much at one time and can concentrate his/her somewhat limited attention to processing manageable size pieces of information or skill" (p. 378). In addition to careful orientation to new material, such techniques as frequent reviewing, providing multiple learning tasks, guided practice, use of engaging and appropriate material, good questioning techniques, and clear explanations that highlight key concepts and make use of appropriate metaphors have been found to help students in both regular and special education settings to understand the content of the lesson (Brophy & Good, 1986; Conoley, 1988; Druian & Butler, 1987; Osborn et al., 1985; Reynolds, 1992; Rosenshine, 1983; Taylor & Valentine, 1985; Williams, 1988; Zigmond et al., 1986).

Related Job Analysis Findings

Wesley et al. (1993) found that this criterion was rated as "moderately important," "very important," or "extremely important" by 100% of those responding and as "very important" or "extremely important" by 95% of those responding. This criterion had a mean rating of 4.54 (on a scale of 0.0 lowest to 5.0 highest) across all respondents. Zero percent of the respondents said that they would not expect this aspect of teaching to have been mastered by the beginning teacher. In an earlier study, Powers (1992) found ratings of "important" or "very important" from 99% of those responding to the July 1991 version of this criterion ("Make content comprehensible to students"). In the spring 1992 survey, the identically worded criterion was rated "important" or "very important" by 99% of the respondents.

Related State Licensing Requirements

States with teacher licensing performance assessment requirements related to this criterion include: Connecticut, Florida, Kentucky, Maine, Mississippi, Missouri, North Carolina, Tennessee, and Utah (Klem, 1992).

Fieldwork Findings

This criterion has been part of the system throughout development. Because of its atypically wide scope, September 1992 revisions of both the description and scoring rules focused on helping to provide an organized way of analyzing evidence in this area. In the spring 1992 pilot studies, paired assessors' ratings were within one-half point of each other for 81.4% of the candidates assessed (Livingston, 1993).

Criterion C3: Encouraging Students to Extend Their Thinking

CRITERION DESCRIPTION. This criterion focuses on the aspects of teaching in any situation that encourage students to develop and have confidence in their own ability to think independently, creatively, or critically. The term "thinking" is used broadly here, and "extending their thinking" does not necessarily imply elaborate exercises, or activities that are foreign to the subject being taught.

Sometimes students do learn content through simple, low-level cognitive processes, for example, by memorizing vocabulary in other languages or procedures for a mathematical operation. More frequently, however, teachers enable students to move beyond the "facts" and extend their thinking, for example, by having them make connections between different events, predict the outcome of a story, or invent another method of solving a problem.

Teachers use many instructional techniques to encourage students to extend their thinking—for example, asking open-ended questions, allowing students adequate time to think about their answers to questions, or assigning tasks in which there is more than one method of completing the task. Through all these strategies, the teacher invites students to extend their thinking.

Nontraditional subject areas also provide opportunities for extending thinking. Solving problems creatively requires thinking, whether the subject area is science, visual art, home economics, shop, or any other area. When the content being studied involves primarily physical skills, extending thinking may become a matter of helping students to recognize the possibilities inherent in skills learned, to integrate skills, or to consider the strategic possibilities in their choice of skills. Similarly, in performance classes, such as drama, extending thinking may involve helping students to integrate performance skills or to understand the relationships between skills or techniques and the performance as a whole.

Many opportunities for students to extend their thinking arise spontaneously in teaching, as when the teacher asks students for their opinions or for alternative explanations. As teachers gain skill, they frequently design an activity or a lesson specifically to encourage students to extend their thinking, as when students are asked to write an essay comparing one author to another, or to consider questions such as why leaves turn brown in the fall, or to offer constructive criticisms of their own or each other's work or performance.

Related Research Literature

Effective teachers provide instruction that encourages students to extend their thinking. The U.S. Department of Education report, *What Works* (1987), found that increases in student achievement are related to questioning that requires students to apply, analyze, synthesize, and evaluate information instead of simply recalling facts.

Goodwin, Sharp, Cloutier & Diamond (1983) suggest that such teachers use questioning strategies that challenge students at several cognitive levels. Ellett (1990) states that "In teaching students to think, the teacher deliberately structures and uses teaching methods and learning tasks that ACTIVELY INVOLVE STUDENTS [original emphasis] in ample opportunities to develop concepts and skills in generating, structuring, transferring and restructuring knowledge. Thinking is an active, cognitive process and represents much more than soliciting information from, or presenting information to students, in its final form. There is a large literature in teaching higher order thinking skills and no particular set of tasks or specific strategies can be prescribed for each context in which teachers function" (p. 47). Marzano, Brandt, Hughes, Jones, Presseisen, Rankin, and Suhor (1988) stress that teachers who want their students to think critically and creatively need to incorporate and cultivate these ways of thinking into their own behavior patterns. Several researchers have found that engaging students in creative thinking is related to higher subsequent student achievement (Dunkin & Biddle, 1974; Rosenshine, 1971). In addition, Rosenshine and Furst (1971) investigated the relationship of teaching behavior to pupil learning. Their review of 50 studies reported a strong positive relationship between higher-order and probing questions and pupil learning. The report also found that students become more competent at solving mathematics problems when teachers guide them through the process and give frequent feedback.

As noted above, Irvine (1990), Levin (1987), Moll (1988), Oakes (1986), and Stage (1989) argue that the lower academic performance of some minority students is, in part, a result of a "watered-down" curriculum that precludes the development of higher-order thinking. They therefore urge teachers of ethnically and linguistically diverse students to be certain to provide instruction that encourages students to extend their thinking.

Related Job Analysis Findings

Wesley et al. (1993) found that this criterion was rated as "moderately important," "very important," or "extremely important" by 96% of those responding and as "very important" or "extremely important" by 80% of those responding. This criterion had a mean rating of 4.12 (on a scale of 0.0 lowest to 5.0 highest) across all respondents. Only two percent of the respondents said that they would not expect this aspect of teaching to have been mastered by the beginning teacher. In an earlier study, Powers (1992) found ratings of "important" or "very important" from 92% of those responding to the July 1991 version of this criterion ("Encourage students to extend their own thinking"). In the spring 1992 study, a similarly worded criterion ("Encourage students to extend their thinking [to think independently, creatively, or critically]) was rated as "important" or "very important" by 93% of the respondents.

Related State Licensing Requirements

States with teacher licensing performance assessment requirements related to this criterion include: Maine, Mississippi, Missouri, New Mexico, Tennessee, and Utah (Klem, 1992). Tracy and Smeaton (1993) cite the closely related "Critical thinking and problem solving" (p. 225) as being required by at least two-thirds of the states included in their study.

Fieldwork Findings

This criterion has been part of the system throughout development. The 1991-92 field studies indicated that it was one of the most difficult for assessors to score and that, at least initially, they felt some uncertainty as to what constitutes evidence of performance in widely varying school contexts. Therefore, the description was completely rewritten for the September 1992 revision, with special attention given to the definition of "thinking" and the criterion's application in areas such as performance-based classes (e.g., art, physical education). The assessor training program was also revised to strengthen this component specifically. In the spring 1992 pilot studies, paired assessors' ratings were within one-half point of each other for 69.0% of the candidates assessed (Livingston, 1993).

Criterion C4: Monitoring Students' Understanding of Content Through a Variety of Means, Providing Feedback to Students to Assist Learning, and Adjusting Learning Activities as the Situation Demands

CRITERION DESCRIPTION.   This criterion refers to the monitoring, feedback, and adjustment that takes place during the lesson. The teacher should monitor the students' understanding of the content throughout the lesson. Monitoring may be accomplished by a variety of means—checking written work, asking questions, paying attention to nonverbal cues from students, and so on. In some specialized situations (e.g., large choir rehearsal), it may be appropriate to monitor groups (e.g., altos) rather than individual students.

In a culturally diverse classroom, especially one that includes students of limited English proficiency, the teacher must be especially sensitive to the verbal and nonverbal signals that each student might use to indicate that he or she is confused or does not understand what is expected. This may require insight into culturally specific ways of expressing understanding and confusion. For example, silence may denote comprehension in one group, but confusion in another.

The teacher should provide specific feedback to reinforce those who are on track and redirect or assist those who need extra help. Feedback can take the form of specific comments to individuals or remarks to groups of students, or it can be nonverbal. Depending on how instruction is organized, feedback can come from sources other than the teacher, such as other students, books, self-checking materials, or the activity itself.

The teacher should use information gained from monitoring students' understanding to assess the effectiveness of the particular instructional approach. As the teacher gains skill, he or she should be able to adjust the learning activities as necessary if they are not working as intended or if the students are having unexpected problems. In addition, the teacher may choose to adjust instruction not because of problems, but because he or she recognizes a "teachable moment" and adjusts instruction in order to capitalize on it.

Monitoring, feedback, and adjustment must take into account all of the students in the class. If a group of students is consistently disregarded, or if a group receives the majority of the teacher's attention and the teacher can give no sound reason for this, then monitoring, feedback, and adjustment are not adequate. In some cases, monitoring may be difficult to observe directly; in such cases, feedback to students or adjustment of the lesson can serve as evidence that monitoring has occurred.

Related Research Literature

Effective teachers monitor student progress in mastering the defined learning goals (Brophy & Good, 1986; Gage, 1978; Good & Grouws, 1975). The U.S. Department of Education report, *What Works* (1987), included the need for constructive feedback from teachers, such as praise and specific suggestions, as one of the characteristics of effective teachers. This educational practice assists student learning and develops self-esteem.

Sanford and Evertson (1980) and Emmer (1982) report that appropriate monitoring of student progress is related to increased student achievement. Monitoring may be conducted by providing feedback, clarifying misconceptions, asking direct questions, and readily adjusting the lesson to meet student needs (Carter et al., 1988; Porter & Brophy, 1987, 1988; Stallings & Kaskowitz, 1974). Teachers whose students demonstrated high on-task rates and academic achievement systematically monitored student academic work and behavior and provided regular feedback about performance and behavior (Evertson & Harris, 1992).

Sigel (1990) reviewed the literature in this area that supports the importance of good questioning techniques to student learning. Effective teaching requires clear and precise formulation of questions, waiting an appropriate interval for a student response, and follow-through using the student's response as a base (p. 85).

Shulman (1987) provides a broad view of student evaluation that illustrates the need for both the ongoing, informal evaluation required in this criterion and the more formal techniques that are reflected in Criterion

A5, "Creating or selecting evaluation strategies that are appropriate for the students and that are aligned with the goals of the lesson." Shulman says: "This process includes the on-line checking for understanding and misunderstanding that a teacher must employ while teaching interactively, as well as the more formal testing and evaluation that teachers do to provide feedback and grades" (p. 18-19). Student evaluation such as checking for student understanding during interactive teaching and testing student understanding at the end of lessons or units is included in Shulman's Model of Pedagogical Reasoning and Action (1987, p.15). Rosenshine and Stevens (1986) report that, in general, researchers have found that when effective teachers teach well-structured subjects, they "…provide a high level of active practice for all students; ask a large number of questions, check for student understanding, and obtain responses from all students" (p. 377).

Studying elementary level mathematics performance, McDonald (1976) and Stallings (1982) reported that student performance is increased by monitoring student work and providing immediate feedback. In addition, Zigmond et al. (1986) have also found that frequent, paced questioning is helpful in monitoring the progress of learning disabled students in learning basic skills.

Related Job Analysis Findings

Wesley et al. (1993) found that this criterion was rated as "moderately important," "very important," or "extremely important" by 94% of those responding and as "very important" or "extremely important" by 82% of those responding. This criterion had a mean rating of 4.05 (on a scale of 0.0 lowest to 5.0 highest) across all respondents. Only five percent of the respondents said that they would not expect this aspect of teaching to have been mastered by the beginning teacher. In an earlier study, Powers (1992) found ratings of "important" or "very important" from 93% of those responding to the July 1991 version of this criterion ("Monitor students' understanding of content through a variety of means, provide feedback to students to assist learning, and adjust learning activities as the situation demands"). In the spring 1992 study, the identically worded criterion was rated as "important" or "very important" by 96% of the respondents.

Related State Licensing Requirements

States with teacher licensing performance assessment requirements related to this criterion include: Connecticut, Florida, Kentucky, Maine, Mississippi, Missouri, New Mexico, Oklahoma, Tennessee, and Utah (Klem, 1992). Tracy and Smeaton (1993) cite the closely related "Monitoring and feedback of student progress," "Student practice and application," and "Evaluation of student progress" (p. 225) as being required by at least two-thirds of the states included in their study.

Fieldwork Findings

This criterion has been part of the system throughout development. In the September 1992 revision, the description was generally amplified and clarified; the scoring rules were simplified. In the spring 1992 pilot studies, paired assessors' ratings were within one-half point of each other for 82.9% of the candidates assessed (Livingston, 1993).

Criterion C5: Using Instructional Time Effectively

CRITERION DESCRIPTION. This criterion refers to the teacher's skill in using time effectively during the lesson. As used here, "instructional" time means time during which content-related teaching and learning take place. "Non-instructional" time, on the other hand, is time spent on activities that are a necessary part of classroom life but don't contribute to learning.

An important aspect of using time effectively is pacing the lesson in ways that are appropriate to the students in the class. In well-paced instruction, the amount of time spent on learning activities is appropriate to the content, the learners, and the situation. If the pace of instruction is too fast, some or all of the students may not be able to understand the content being taught. When lessons are paced too slowly, students may become bored and student engagement may decline. Digressions from the planned activities do not constitute a waste of time if they result in valuable learning; digressions that simply wander into irrelevant topics for substantial periods of time should be avoided. If a lesson or learning activity is completed more quickly than the teacher anticipated, he or she should provide the students with meaningful and relevant work or activities for the remaining instructional time.

Using time effectively also implies making sure that time spent on necessary, but *noninstructional*, processes is minimized. Therefore, effective classroom routines and procedures for such noninstructional processes as taking roll and distributing materials contribute positive evidence for this criterion since they enable the teacher to spend more class time on learning activities. As the teacher gains skill, her or his sense of appropriate pacing should become more accurate, and the efficiency with which noninstructional routines are conducted should increase. Time should not be considered wasted if the reasons for the problem (for example, a lengthy interruption via a PA system) are outside the teacher's control.

Related Research Literature

According to Brophy (1987): "Research on teaching has established that the key to successful classroom management (and to successful instruction as well) is the teacher's ability to maximize the time that students spend actively engaged in worthwhile academic activities (attending to lessons, working on assignments) and to minimize the time that they spend waiting for activities to get started, making transitions between activities, sitting with nothing to do, or engaging in misconduct" (p. 5). The U.S. Department of Education report, *What Works* (1987), cited managing classroom time as an important factor in effective teaching and learning. The report found that the amount of time students spend actively engaged in learning is positively related to achievement and that the amount of time available for learning is related to the instructional and management skills of the classroom teacher.

Effective teachers plan, organize, and carry out lessons so that maximum time is spent on instruction (Anderson, 1986; Emans & Milburn, 1989; Emmer, Evertson, & Anderson, 1980; Evertson & Emmer, 1982; Gage, 1978; Ysseldyke et al., 1987). In reviewing the research on effective teaching, Brophy & Good (1986) report that, "Engagement rates depend on the teacher's ability to organize and manage the classroom as an efficient learning environment where academic activities run smoothly, transitions are brief and orderly, and little time is spent getting organized or dealing with inattention or resistance" (p. 360).

Furthermore, it appears that the amount of time students spend engaged in the lesson is related to increased student achievement (Brophy & Good, 1986; Conoley, 1988; Evertson, 1989; Gettinger, 1986; Karweit, 1988). Other studies have supported the concept of establishing a classroom management system, preferably at the beginning of the school year, resulting in higher task engagement, less inappropriate behavior, and higher academic success (Doyle, 1990; Emmer & Aussiker, 1990; Evertson, Emmer, Sanford, Clements and Martin, 1983; Emmer et al., 1982; Evertson, 1985, 1989). These findings also hold true for learning disabled and linguistically and culturally diverse student populations (Zigmond et al., 1986; Arreaga-Mayer & Greenwood, 1986).

Related Job Analysis Findings

Wesley et al. (1993) found that this criterion was rated as "moderately important," "very important," or "extremely important" by 97% of those responding and as "very important" or "extremely important" by 86% of those responding. This criterion had a mean rating of 4.20 (on a scale of 0.0 lowest to 5.0 highest) across all respondents. Only two percent of the respondents said that they would not expect this aspect of teaching to have been mastered by the beginning teacher. In an earlier study, Powers (1992) found ratings of "important" or "very important" from 93% of those responding to the July 1991 version of this criterion ("Use instructional time effectively and efficiently"). In the spring 1992 study, a similarly worded criterion ("Use instructional time effectively") was rated as "important" or "very important" by 95% of the respondents.

Related State Licensing Requirements

States with teacher licensing performance assessment requirements related to this criterion include: Connecticut, Florida, Kentucky, Maine, Mississippi, Missouri, New Mexico, North Carolina, Oklahoma, Tennessee, and Utah (Klem, 1992). Tracy and Smeaton (1993) cite the closely related "Management of class time" and "Student practice and application" (p. 225) as being required by at least two-thirds of the states included in their study.

Fieldwork Findings

This criterion has been part of the system since the summer of 1991. In the September 1992 revision, the description was amplified, with particular attention to explaining what is meant by "noninstructional procedures," to distinguish them from the instructional procedures covered in criterion C1 ("Making learning goals and instructional procedures clear to students"). In the spring 1992 pilot studies, paired assessors' ratings were within one-half point of each other for 90.9% of the candidates assessed (Livingston, 1993).

DOMAIN D: TEACHER PROFESSIONALISM

Teachers must be able to evaluate their own instructional effectiveness in order to plan specific future lessons for particular classes and to improve their teaching over time. They should be able to discuss the degree to which different aspects of a lesson were successful in terms of instructional approaches, student responses, and learning outcomes. Teachers should be able to explain how they will proceed to work toward learning for *all* students. The professional responsibilities of all teachers, including beginning teachers, also include sharing appropriate information with other professionals and with families in ways that support the learning of diverse student populations.

Domain D consists of the following four criteria.

Criterion D1: Reflecting on the Extent to Which the Learning Goals Were Met

CRITERION DESCRIPTION. Teaching extends far beyond interaction with students in the classroom, and includes reflection both before and after classroom instruction. Teachers must be able to reflect on classroom events, both in order to plan next steps for individuals or groups of students and in order to improve their teaching skills over time. Toward these ends, this criterion focuses on the teacher's skill in determining the extent to which the students in the class achieved the learning goals. In order to plan the next lessons for this group of students, the teacher must know the extent to which individuals and groups of students achieved the goals for this lesson. For example, if a certain group did not understand a concept, the teacher must know, and be prepared with, a plan—to be implemented subsequently—to remedy the situation.

In addition, teachers must be able to analyze their teaching of a lesson in terms of both successes and areas needing improvement. Many lessons—particularly those being taught for the first time—do not proceed exactly as planned. By consciously reflecting on these lessons and analyzing their strong and weak features, teachers are able to learn from their experiences and improve their skills.

In stating what they plan to do subsequently with a group of students, based on what occurred in the observed lesson, teachers provide evidence of their skill in using the results from one lesson to plan for the future. By describing how they might teach the same lesson again, teachers demonstrate their skill in constructively critiquing their own performance. As teachers gain skill in reflection, they can support their judgments with references to specific events in the classroom. If the lesson had more than one goal, the teacher may be able to discuss in comparative terms the degree to which the students as a group achieved the various goals. They may also be able to make and support judgments with respect to the learning of particular individuals or groups of students.

Related Research Literature

Jones (1992) and Reynolds (1992) indicate the considerable support that exists in the educational research literature for the effective teacher's ability to reflect on the extent to which instructional goals were met in order to fine-tune teaching. The research and practice consensus on this topic is unusually strong, but this is clearly an area where the research base is still in a highly active and evolving state. A significant proportion of the research in this area is qualitative in nature, and links teacher reflectiveness to teacher improvement and student learning through logical argument rather than through empirical data.

Frequently cited research in this area includes studies by Zeichner and his colleagues (e.g., Zeichner & Tabachnick, 1991) on the wide ramifications of reflective practice. Recognizing that teacher reflection is not exclusively a private cognitive act, some studies link research on teacher reflection with research on sharing professional experiences among teachers (e.g., Ross & Regan, 1993). Ellwein, Graue, and Comfort (1990) and Borko and her colleagues (Borko, Lalik, & Tomchin, 1987; Borko, Livingston, McCaleb & Mauro, 1988; Borko & Livingston, 1989) have also investigated this area with respect to student teachers' reflections. It is generally conceded that novice teachers are sharply differentiated from experts by their lesser ability to profit from reflection on their own teaching. Reynolds (1992, p. 25) sums this up as follows:

Competent teachers evaluate their own teaching effectiveness by reflecting on their own actions and student responses in order to improve their practice. Beginning teachers do reflect on their practice, but their reflections appear to be less focused than experienced teachers' reflections...Reflection may help the beginning teacher develop schemata for making meaning out of classroom experiences.

Research on teacher thinking encompasses both research on teacher reflection and research on teachers' beliefs, which includes a sense of efficacy (Criterion D2, below). Pajares (1992) provides a useful overview of this broader area.

Colton and Sparks-Langer have conducted a program of research on the teachers' role in a reflective learning community (Colton & Sparks-Langer, 1992, 1993; Sparks-Langer, Simmons, Pasch, Colton, & Starko, 1990) that links this criterion with D4, "Building professional relationships with colleagues to share teaching insights and to coordinate learning activities for students."

For additional recent studies on the value of teacher reflection, see Calderhead (1989), Grimmett & Erickson (1988), Kemmis (1987), Schön (1987), and Weiss & Louden (1989). Note also that with respect to accomplished teaching practice, the National Board for Professional Teaching Standards (1991), as one of its five major propositions that guide its standard-setting and assessment work, includes as its fourth proposition: "Teachers think systematically about their practice and learn from experience" (p. 24).

Related Job Analysis Findings

Wesley et al. (1993) found that this criterion was rated as "moderately important," "very important," or "extremely important" by 96% of those responding and as "very important" or "extremely important" by 73% of those responding. This criterion had a mean rating of 3.92 (on a scale of 0.0 lowest to 5.0 highest) across all respondents. Only one percent of the respondents said that they would not expect this aspect of teaching to have been mastered by the beginning teacher. In an earlier study, Powers (1992) found ratings of "important" or "very important" from 95% of those responding to the July 1991 version of this criterion ("Reflect on the extent to which instructional goals were met"). In the spring 1992 study, a similarly worded criterion ("Reflect on the extent to which the instructional goals were met and explain how insights gained from instructional experience can be used subsequently") was rated as "important" or "very important" by 82% of the respondents.

Related State Licensing Requirements

States with teacher licensing performance assessment requirements related to this criterion include: Connecticut, Maine, Mississippi, Oklahoma, Tennessee, and Utah (Klem, 1992).

Fieldwork Findings

This criterion has been part of the system since the spring of 1991. In the September 1992 revision, the description was amplified, particularly to acknowledge explicitly that an observed lesson may not go smoothly, and to distinguish the ability to recognize and reflect on what actually occurred. In the spring 1992 pilot studies, paired assessors' ratings were within one-half point of each other for 93.0% of the candidates assessed (Livingston, 1993).

Criterion D2: Demonstrating a Sense of Efficacy

CRITERION DESCRIPTION.   A teacher who has a sense of efficacy attributes the degree of students' success in meeting learning goals to factors within the classroom rather than to factors outside it. This criterion focuses on the ways in which teachers demonstrate and act on that belief.

Teachers with a high degree of efficacy regard student difficulties in learning as challenges to their own creativity and ingenuity. They actively search for better techniques to help students learn. Thus, a teacher with a high degree of efficacy is not expected to know all the answers to reaching every student, but he or she will persist in looking for alternatives. On the other hand, teachers with little sense of efficacy tend to use factors such as the school administration, excessive television viewing, students' families, or the students themselves as excuses for not persisting in efforts to help students learn.

Teachers with a high sense of efficacy are not expected to have a complete plan to deal with every student's difficulties in learning, particularly immediately after an observed lesson. However, these teachers are prepared with several possible actions and convey a sense of commitment to persisting in the search for an effective approach so every student can meet the learning goals.

As teachers gain skill in this area, they become more resourceful and their repertoire of possible approaches or actions to try broadens.

Related Research Literature

Jones (1992) cites the links established in the process-product research literature between the teacher's efficacy and student learning. As noted above, the research base for this area has also been linked to the research on teacher reflection (e.g., Ross & Regan, 1993). Smylie (1988) and Stein and Wang (1988) also cite a sense of efficacy as a critical factor in the development of teacher effectiveness.

Pajares (1992) provides a good overview of the teacher belief area (which includes a teacher's sense of efficacy) and builds on an earlier comprehensive review on this topic by Clark and Peterson (1986). Pajares, in describing some semantic and conceptual difficulties in research in this area, points out that knowledge and beliefs are "inextricably intertwined" (p. 325), but that "Few would argue [against the point of view] that the beliefs teachers hold influence their perceptions and judgments, which, in turn, affect their behavior in the classroom, or that understanding the belief structures of teachers and teacher candidates is essential to improving their professional preparation and teaching practices." (p. 307). Porter and Brophy (1987, 1988), in summarizing a long program of research conducted by the Institute for Research on Teaching, conclude that effective teachers accept personal responsibility for pupil learning and behavior. They engage in corrective, problem-solving approaches with failing pupils rather than punishing them for their shortcomings. Pajares also quotes Arthur Combs as follows: "Perhaps the most important single cause of a person's success or failure educationally has to do with the question of what he believes about himself." This statement reflects the very strong and consistent support in the psychological literature for a sense of efficacy as key to understanding social cognition generally, and teacher effectiveness specifically.

New research on teachers' sense of efficacy stresses multiple methods of data gathering, including observations and self-reports, and the importance of including qualitative methodologies is stressed by some researchers (e.g., Schunk, 1991). Others point to the need for further research on pre-service teachers to guide teacher education (e.g., Ashton & Webb, 1986; Woolfolk & Hoy, 1990).

Note also that with respect to accomplished teaching practice, the National Board for Professional Teaching Standards (1991), as one of its five major propositions that guide its standard-setting and assessment work, includes as its first proposition: "Teachers are committed to students and their learning" (p. 17).

Related Job Analysis Findings

Wesley et al. (1993) found that this criterion was rated as "moderately important," "very important," or "extremely important" by 93% of those responding and as "very important" or "extremely important" by 66% of those responding. This criterion had a mean rating of 3.69 (on a scale of 0.0 lowest to 5.0 highest) across all respondents. Only three percent of the respondents said that they would not expect this aspect of teaching to have been mastered by the beginning teacher. In an earlier study, Powers (1992) found ratings of "important" or "very important" from 86% of those responding to the July 1991 version of this criterion ("Demonstrate acceptance of responsibility for student learning"). In the spring 1992 study, a similarly worded criterion ("Demonstrate a sense of efficacy and acceptance of responsibility for student learning") was rated as "important" or "very important" by 81% of the respondents.

Related State Licensing Requirements

States with teacher licensing performance assessment requirements related to this criterion include: Connecticut, Mississippi, Missouri, Oklahoma, Tennessee, and Utah (Klem, 1992).

Fieldwork Findings

This criterion has been part of the system since the spring of 1991. Throughout the pilot studies, it was an exceptionally difficult criterion for assessors to score, although there was a high level of agreement that it embodies important concepts. In the September 1992 revision, the description was completely rewritten to focus on an explanation of efficacy and how it can be evidenced. The revision of the scoring rules resulted in a change from a focus on abstract qualities to a much more concrete focus on how teachers work or propose to work with actual students. In the spring 1992 pilot studies, paired assessors' ratings were within one-half point of each other for 83.3% of the candidates assessed (Livingston, 1993).

Criterion D3: Building Professional Relationships With Colleagues to Share Teaching Insights and to Coordinate Learning Activities for Students

CRITERION DESCRIPTION. This criterion focuses on two distinct, though related, aspects of a teacher's professional relationships with colleagues. The first of these is seeking help from other professionals on matters related to learning and instruction or to other concerns related to teaching. For example, the teacher should know who in the school is experienced in working with students of the same level or in the same subject area, and should be aware of other people in the school or district who can help the teacher improve his or her instructional skills. The teacher should also be aware of others—for example, librarians or specialist teachers—who can provide assistance with curricular materials or other resources to enrich the learning experience for students.

Secondly, the teacher should be aware of how, and with whom, he or she could or should coordinate plans, schedules, and resources for the benefit of the entire class or individual students. As teachers gain skill, they are able to collaborate effectively with colleagues. Examples of such collaboration might include working with other teachers to design integrated lessons or units, coordinating plans with specialists such as ESL teachers, and maintaining close contact with special education teachers for mainstreamed students, and so on. Teachers who team-teach should demonstrate knowledge of how to coordinate activities with colleagues other than the team-teaching partner.

Related Research Literature

As Jones (1992) indicates, the teacher practice literature has long recognized and supported the importance of building professional relationships with colleagues to improve practice and enhance student learning. She quotes from the U.S. Department of Education's *What works: Research about teaching and learning* (1987): "Students benefit academically when their teachers share ideas, cooperate in activities, and assist one another's intellectual growth... Good instruction flourishes when teachers collaborate... (p.80)."

Little (1992) also addresses the issue of equity in the classroom and its relationship to teacher collaborations. She notes that the most promising of these efforts engage teachers collectively in studying classroom practices in ways that sometimes lead to more systemic changes at the school level (page 2), and thus lead to broader impacts on learning, as well as to changes for individual students.

Researchers have reported on the consistency of this view (e.g., Dill and Associates, 1990; Griffin, 1986). Griffin characterizes the effective teacher as one who "...interacts with students, colleagues, and community members purposefully and effectively. The individual sees teaching as more than meeting with students and *works with peers to identify and act on problems in the classrooms and schools* [emphasis added]." As noted above, recent research recognizes the close links between these professional relationships and teacher reflectiveness (e.g., Ross & Regan, 1993). This vein of research makes extensive use of actual classroom experiences and also exploits this set of theoretical connections.

As noted above, the research base for this criterion has close ties to the research base on teacher reflection (e.g., Ross & Regan, 1993; Schön, 1987). Collaborating with colleagues in reflective activities also enhances teacher effectiveness. Note also that with respect to accomplished teaching practice, the National Board for Professional Teaching Standards (1991), as one of its five major propositions that guide its standard-setting and assessment work, includes as its fifth proposition: "Teachers are members of learning communities" (p. 26).

Related Job Analysis Findings

Wesley et al. (1993) found that this criterion was rated as "moderately important," "very important," or "extremely important" by 94% of those responding and as "very important" or "extremely important" by 68% of those responding. This criterion had a mean rating of 3.81 (on a scale of 0.0 lowest to 5.0 highest) across all respondents. Only three percent of the respondents said that they would not expect this aspect of teaching to have been mastered by the beginning teacher.

In an earlier study, Powers (1992) found ratings of "important" or "very important" from 84% of the fall 1991 sample of those responding to this criterion, and 76% from the spring 1992 sample.

Related State Licensing Requirements

States with teacher licensing performance assessment requirements related to this criterion include: Missouri, Oklahoma, Tennessee, and Utah (Klem, 1992).

Fieldwork Findings

This criterion has been part of the system since the spring of 1991. In the September 1992 revision, the description of this criterion was amplified and examples were added. In the spring 1992 pilot studies, paired assessors' ratings were within one-half point of each other for 86.4% of the candidates assessed (Livingston, 1993).

Criterion D4: Communicating With Parents or Guardians About Student Learning

CRITERION DESCRIPTION. This criterion focuses on the teacher's contacts with the parents or guardians of students. The nature of communications with parents or guardians regarding the school success of their children will vary significantly with age or grade level and the subject being taught. Potential forms of communication might include, for example, scheduled conferences with parents, telephone calls or written notes about positive events as well as individual students' problems, or class newsletters. For teachers who have instructional contact with large numbers of students, the realistic possibilities will be somewhat more limited than for teachers in self-contained classrooms. Even undifferentiated means of communication—for example, notification of special events such as plays, exhibitions, sports events—can constitute communication with students' parents or guardians.

In all cases, such communication should be handled in a nonthreatening way that is respectful of the cultural diversity in the community. For example, teachers should be sensitive to the effects that a call to a parent at work could have and should be aware of whether communication exclusively in English is reasonable.

As teachers gain skill, their familiarity with forms of communication should broaden, and they should become more knowledgeable about which forms are likely to be effective in a particular situation.

Related Research Literature

The effectiveness of parent-teacher involvement in student learning is well established. A widely cited report by the U. S. Department of Education, *What works: Research about Teaching and Learning* (1987), points to parent involvement as a critical component of effective educational practice, and Jones (1992) and Cruickshank (1990) cite the department as suggesting that, in general, student learning is enhanced when teachers work at parent involvement. Jones notes that minority children in particular often experience discontinuity between their home and school experiences and that teachers need to be in communication with parents as an important avenue to learning for these students (Cazden, 1986; Hilliard, 1989; Irvine, 1989; Michaels, 1981). This is a point echoed by Villegas (1992) in an extensive literature review and description of the broader concept of culturally responsive teaching. Anderson (1991) provides an analysis of the general cognitive theoretical rationale for this effect.

In a format intended for use by practicing teachers, Powell, Casanova, and Berliner (1991) provide an up-to-date review of the research on parental involvement and its effect on student learning. In this set of readings, they establish that parental involvement is intimately associated with academic achievement and that there are a variety of ways in which teachers can establish and enhance such involvement.

McDiarmid (1991) links the concept of parental involvement with teachers' "need to know what kind of knowledge, skills, and commitments are valued in the learners' cultures. Such knowledge is critical to developing representations of subject matter..." (p. 267).

There are other aspects of parental involvement to be considered as well. Jones (1992) also cites Darling-Hammond (1989) on the rights of parents as decision makers in their children's education. Such rights are logically of considerable importance in teacher licensing assessments, which are intended to protect the public.

Related Job Analysis Findings

Wesley et al. (1993) found that this criterion was rated as "moderately important," "very important," or "extremely important" by 97% of those responding and as "very important" or "extremely important" by 82% of those responding. This criterion had a mean rating of 4.16 (on a scale of 0.0 lowest to 5.0 highest) across all respondents. Only one percent of the respondents said that they would not expect this aspect of teaching to have been mastered by the beginning teacher. In an earlier study, Powers (1992) found ratings of "important" or "very important" from 84% of those responding to the July 1991 version of this criterion ("Communicate with families regarding student learning and, where appropriate, interact effectively with the community"). In the spring 1992 study, a similarly worded criterion ("Communicate with families regarding student learning") was rated as "important" or "very important" by 81% of the respondents.

Related State Licensing Requirements

States with teacher licensing performance assessment requirements related to this criterion include: Missouri, Oklahoma, Tennessee, and Utah (Klem, 1992).

Fieldwork Findings

This criterion has been part of the system since the spring of 1991. In the September 1992 revision, the description was amplified. In the spring 1992 pilot studies, paired assessors' ratings were within one-half point of each other for 84.1% of the candidates assessed (Livingston, 1993).

CONCLUSION

The development of the assessment criteria for the PRAXIS III: Classroom Performance Assessments was the result of a lengthy and intensive process of research and fieldwork. The final version of the criteria is well supported by the research literature in education and psychology. In addition, thousands of practicing teachers and other educators contributed their professional expertise to the development of these criteria through job analyses, fieldwork, and research. Further experience with the operational use of the criteria and new research findings will no doubt shed further light on the meaning and significance of these important aspects of teaching.

REFERENCES

Adams, R., & Biddle, B. (1970). *Realities of teaching: Explorations with videotape.* New York: Holt, Rinehart, & Winston.

Anderson, A. B. (1991). Teaching children: What teachers should know. In M. M. Kennedy (Ed.), *Teaching academic subjects to diverse learners* (pp. 203-217). New York: Teachers College Press.

Anderson, C. W., & Smith, E. L. (1987). Teaching science. In V. Koehler (Ed.), *The educator's handbook: A research perspective* (pp. 84-111). New York: Longman.

Anderson, L. W. (1986, April). Research on teaching and educational effectiveness. *National Association of Secondary School Principals Curriculum Report, 15*(4, entire issue). (ERIC Document Reproduction Service No. ED 269 868)

Anderson, L., Evertson, C. M., & Emmer, E. L. (1979). Dimensions in classroom management derived from recent research. In S. Dasho (Chair), *Perspectives on Classroom Management Research.* Symposium conducted at the annual meeting of the American Educational Research Association, San Francisco. (ERIC Document Reproduction Service No. ED 175 860)

Armento, B. (1977). Teacher behaviors related to student achievement on a social science concept test. *Journal of Teacher Education, 28*(3), 46-52.

Arreaga-Mayer, C., & Greenwood, C. (1986). Environmental variables affecting the school achievement of culturally and linguistically different learners: An instructional perspective. *NABE: Journal for the National Association of Bilingual Education, 10*(2), 113-35.

Ashton, P. T., & Webb, R. B. (1986). *Making a difference: Teachers' sense of efficacy and student achievement.* New York: Longman.

Austria, R. H. (1993). *PRAXIS III: Classroom Performance Assessments, the Delaware collaboration, March 1991-August 1992.* Princeton, NJ: Educational Testing Service.

Baker, S. H. (1973). Teacher effectiveness and social class as factors in teacher expectancy effects on pupils' scholastic achievement (Doctoral Dissertation, Clark University, 1973). *Dissertation Abstracts International, 34,* 2376A.

Borko, H., Lalik, R., & Tomchin, E. (1987). Student teachers' understandings of successful and unsuccessful teaching. *Teaching and Teacher Education, 3*(2), 77-90.

Borko, H., Livingston, C., McCaleb, J., & Mauro, L. (1988). Student teachers' planning and post-lesson reflections: Patterns and implications of teacher preparation. In J. Calderhead (Ed.), *Teachers' professional learning* (pp. 65-83). Philadelphia: Falmer Press.

Borko, H., & Livingston, C. (1989). Cognition and improvisation: Differences in mathematics instruction by expert and novice teachers. *American Educational Research Journal, 26*(4), 473-498.

Brophy, J. (1987). *Educating teachers about managing classrooms and students* (Occasional paper No. 115). East Lansing, MI: Institute for Research on Teaching.

Brophy, J. (1983). Classroom organization and management. *Elementary School Journal, 83*, 265-286.

Brophy, J. E., & Good, T. L. (1986). Teacher behavior and student achievement. In M. C. Wittrock (Ed.), *Handbook of research on teaching* (3rd ed., pp. 328-375). New York: Macmillan.

Brophy, J. E., & Putnam, J. G. (1979). *Classroom management in the elementary grades: a literature review.* East Lansing, MI: Institute for Research on Teaching, Michigan State University.

Calderhead, J. (1989). Reflective teaching and teacher education. *Teaching and Teacher Education, 5*(1), 43-51.

Carter, K., Cushing, K., Sabers, D., Stein, P., & Berliner, D. (1988). Expert-novice differences in perceiving and processing visual classroom information. *Journal of Teacher Education, 39*(1), 25-31.

Cazden, C. (1986). Classroom discourse. In M. Wittrock (Ed.), *Handbook of research on teaching,* (3rd ed., pp. 434-463). New York: Macmillan.

Cazden, C., & Mehan, H. (1989). Principles from sociology and anthropology: Context, code, classroom, and culture. In M. C. Reynolds (Ed.), *Knowledge base for the beginning teacher* (pp. 47-57). New York: Pergamon.

Clark, C. M. (1993). What makes a good teacher? *Doubts & Certainties: A Forum on School Transformation from the NEA National Center for Innovation, 7*(4), 1-5.

Clark, C. M., & Peterson, P. L. (1986). Teachers' thought processes. In M. C. Wittrock (Ed.), *Handbook of research on teaching* (3rd ed., pp. 255-295). New York: Macmillan.

Clark, C. M., & Yinger, R. J. (1977). Research on teacher thinking. *Curriculum Inquiry, 7,* 279-304.

Clark, C. M., & Yinger, R. J. (1979). *Three studies of Teacher Planning.* East Lansing, MI: Michigan State University Institute of Research on Teaching, Research Series No. 55

Colton, A. B., & Sparks-Langer, G. M. (1992). Restructuring student teaching experiences. In C. Glickman (Ed.), *Supervision in transition.* Alexandria, VA: Association for Supervision and Curriculum Development.

Colton, A. B., & Sparks-Langer, G. M. (1993). A conceptual framework to guide the development of teacher reflection and decision making. *Journal of Teacher Education, 44*(1), 45-54.

Conoley, J. (1988, January). Positive classroom ecology. *Bios,* pp. 2-7.

Cooper, H., & Good, T. L. (1983). *Pygmalion grows up: Studies in the expectation communication process.* New York: Longman.

Corno, L., & Snow, R. E. (1986). Adapting teaching to individual differences among learners. In M. C. Wittrock (Ed.), *Handbook of research on teaching* (3rd ed., pp. 605-629). New York: Macmillan.

Cruickshank, D. R. (1990). *Research that informs teachers and teacher educators.* Bloomington, IN: Phi Delta Kappa Educational Foundation.

Cryan, J. (1986). Evaluation: Plague or promise? *Childhood Education, 62*(5), 344-350.

Darling-Hammond, L. (1989). Accountability for professional practice. *Teachers College Record, 91*(1), 59-80.

Delpit, L. D. (1988). The silenced dialogue: Power and pedagogy in educating other people's children. *Harvard Educational Review, 58*(3), 280-298.

Diaz, S., Moll, L.C., & Mehan, H. (1986). Sociocultural resources in instruction: A context-specific approach. In California State Department of Education, *Beyond language: Social and cultural factors in schooling language minority students* (pp. 187-230). Los Angeles, CA: California State University Evaluation, Dissemination, and Assessment Center.

Dill, D. D., and Associates [sic]. (1990). *What teachers need to know: The knowledge, skills, and values essential to good teaching.* San Francisco: Jossey-Bass.

Doyle, W. (1986). Classroom organization and management. In M. C. Wittrock (Ed.), *Handbook of research on teaching* (3rd ed., pp. 392-431). New York: Macmillan.

Druian, G., & Butler, J. (1987). *School improvement research series. Research you can use.* Portland, OR: Northwest Regional Educational Laboratory. (ERIC Document Reproduction Service No. ED 291 145).

Dunkin, M., & Biddle, B. (1974). *The study of teaching.* New York: Holt, Rinehart & Winston.

Dwyer, C. A. (1991). Measurement and research issues in teacher assessment. *Educational Psychologist, 26*(1), 3-22.

Dwyer, C. A. (1993). Teaching and diversity: Meeting the challenges for innovative teacher assessments. *Journal of Teacher Education, 44*(2), 119-129.

Dwyer, C. A., & Villegas, A. M. (1993). *Guiding conceptions and assessment principles for The PRAXIS Series: Professional Assessments for Beginning Teachers*® (Research Rep. No. 93-17). Princeton, NJ: Educational Testing Service.

Edmonds, R., & Frederickson, N. (1978). *Search for effective schools: The identification and analysis of city schools that are instructionally effective for poor children.* Cambridge, MA: Harvard University Center for Policy Studies.

Ellett, C. (1990). *A new generation of classroom-based assessments of teaching and learning: Concepts, issues and controversies from pilots of the Louisiana STAR.* Baton Rouge, LA: College of Education, Louisiana State University.

Ellwein, M. C., Graue, M. E., & Comfort, R. E. (1990). Talking about instruction: Student teachers' reflections on success and failure in the classroom. *Journal of Teacher Education, 41*(4), 3-14.

Emans, R., & Milburn, C. (1989). *The knowledge base of teaching: A review and commentary of process-product research.* Vermillion, SD: The University of South Dakota School of Education.

Emmer, E. T. (1982, July). *Management strategies in elementary school classrooms* (R&D Reproduction Service No. 6052). Austin, TX: The University of Texas at Austin, Research and Development Center for Teacher Education.

Emmer, E. T., & Aussiker, A. (1990). School and classroom discipline programs: How well do they work? In O. C. Moles (Ed.), *Student discipline strategies.* Albany, NY: State University of New York Press.

Emmer, E. T., Evertson, C. M., & Anderson, L. M. (1980). Effective classroom management at the beginning of the school year. *The Elementary School Journal, 80*(5), 219-231.

Emmer, E. T., Evertson, C. M., Sanford, J. P., Clements, B. S., & Worsham, M. E. (1989). *Classroom management for secondary teachers* (2nd ed.). Englewood Cliffs, NJ: Prentice-Hall.

Emmer, E. T., Sanford, J. P., Clements, B. S., & Martin, J. (1982). *Improving classroom management and organization in junior high schools: An experiential investigation* (R&D Report No. 6153). Austin, TX: The University of Texas at Austin, Research and Development Center for Teacher Education.

Englemann, S. (1991) Teachers, schemata, and instruction. In M. M. Kennedy (Ed.), *Teaching academic subjects to diverse learners* (pp. 218-233). New York: Teachers College Press.

Evertson, C. M. (1985). Training teachers in classroom management: An experimental study in secondary school classrooms. *Journal of Educational Research, 79*(1), 51-57.

Evertson, C. M. (1989). Improving classroom management: A school-based program for beginning the year. *Journal of Educational Research, 83*(2), 82-90.

Evertson, C., Anderson, C. H., Anderson, L. M., & Brophy, J. E. (1980). Relationships between classroom behaviors and student outcomes in junior high mathematics and English classes. *American Educational Research Journal, 17,* 43-60.

Evertson, C. M., & Emmer, E. T. (1982). Effective management at the beginning of the school year in junior high school classes. *Journal of Educational Psychology, 74*(4), 485-498.

Evertson, C. M., Emmer, E. T., Sanford, J. P., & Clements, B. S. (1983). Improving classroom management: An experiment in elementary school classrooms. *Elementary School Journal, 84,* 173-188.

Evertson, C. M., Emmer, E. T., Sanford, J. P., Clements, B. S., & Martin, J. (1983 March). *Improving junior high classroom management.* Paper presented at the annual meeting of the American Educational Research Association, Montreal.

Evertson, C. M., & Harris, A. H. (1992). What we know about managing classrooms. *Educational Leadership, 49*(7), 74-78.

Floden, R. E. (1991). What teachers need to know about learning. In M. M. Kennedy (Ed.), *Teaching academic subjects to diverse learners* (pp. 181-202). New York: Teachers College Press.

Floden, R., Buchmann, M., & Schwille, J. (1987). Breaking with everyday experience. *Teachers College Record, 88*, 485-506.

Fogarty, J., Wang, M., & Creek, R. (1983). A descriptive study of experienced and novice teachers' interactive instructional thoughts and actions. *Journal of Educational Research, 77*(1), 22-32.

Fraser, B. J. (1986). *Classroom environment*. London: Groom Helm.

Gage, N. L. (1974). Evaluating ways to help teachers to behave desirably. In *Competency assessment research and evaluation: A report of a national conference, March 12-15, 1974*. Houston, TX: University of Houston.

Gage, N. L. (November, 1978). The yield of research in teaching. *Phi Delta Kappan, 60*, 229-235.

Gallimore, R. (1985, May). *The accommodation of instruction to cultural differences*. Paper presented at the University of California Conference on the Underachievement of Linguistic Minorities, Lake Tahoe, CA.

Gettinger, M. (1986). Issues and trends in academic engaged time of students. *Special Services in the Schools, 2*(4), 1-17.

Glaser, R. (1984). Education and thinking: The role of knowledge. *American Psychologist, 39*, 91-104.

Good, T. L. (1990). Building the knowledge base of teaching. In D. D. Dill and Associates [sic], *What teachers need to know: The knowledge, skills, and values essential to good teaching* (pp. 17-75). San Francisco: Jossey-Bass.

Good, T. L., & Brophy, J. E. (1984). *Looking in classrooms* (3rd ed.). New York: Harper & Row.

Good, T. L., & Brophy, J. E. (1986). *Educational psychology: A realistic approach* (3rd ed.). New York: Longman.

Good, T. L., & Grouws, D. (1975). *Process-product relationships in 4th-grade mathematics classes*. Columbia, MO: University of Missouri College of Education.

Goodwin, S. S., Sharp, G. W., Cloutier, E. F., & Diamond, N. A. (1983). Effective classroom questioning. Paper identified by the Task Force on establishing a National Clearinghouse of Materials Developed for Teaching Assistant (TA) Training. (ERIC Document Reproduction Service No. ED 285 497)

Goss, S. S., & Ingersoll, G. M. (1981). *Management of disruptive and off-task behaviors: selected resources.* Washington, DC: ERIC Clearinghouse on Teacher Education. (ERIC Document Reproduction Service No. SP 017 373).

Grant, C. A. (1991). Culture and teaching: What do teachers need to know? In M. M. Kennedy (Ed.), *Teaching academic subjects to diverse learners* (pp. 237-256). New York: Teachers College Press.

Griffin, G. (1986). Clinical teacher education. In J. Hoffman & S. Edwards (Eds.), *Reality and reform in clinical teacher education* (pp.1-23). New York: Random House.

Grimmett, P., & Erickson, G. (Eds.). (1988). *Reflection in teacher education.* New York: Teachers College Press.

Haertel, G., Walberg, H. J., & Haertel, E. (1981). Sociopsychological environments and learning. *British Educational Research Journal, 7,* 27-36.

Heath, S. B. (1983). *Ways with words: Language, life and work in communities and classrooms.* London: Cambridge.

Heath, S. B. (1983). Questioning at home and in school: A comparative study. In G. Spindler (Ed.), *Doing ethnography: Educational anthropology in action* (pp. 102-131). New York: Holt, Rinehart, & Winston.

Herman, S. H., & Tramontana, J. (1971). Instructions and group versus individual reinforcement in modifying disruptive group behavior. *Journal of Applied Behavior Analysis, 4*(2), 113-119.

Hilliard, A., G. (1989, January). Teachers and cultural style in a pluralistic society. *NEA Today,* 65-69.

Hohn, R. (1986, October). *Research on contextual effects and effective teaching.* Paper presented at the Midwestern Educational Research Association Conference, Chicago, IL. (ERIC Document Reproduction Service No. ED 287 853).

Holliday, B. G. (1985). Differential effects of children's self-perceptions and teachers' perceptions on black children's academic achievement. *Journal of Negro Education, 54,* 71-81.

Hollins, E. (1989). *A conceptual framework for selecting instructional approaches and materials for inner-city Black youngsters.* Sacramento, CA: California Curriculum Commission.

Irvine, J. J. (1989). *Black students and school failure.* New York: Greenwood Press.

Irvine, J. J. (1990, May). *Beyond role models: The influence of black teachers on black students*. Paper presented at Educational Testing Service, Princeton, NJ.

Jones, J. (1992). *PRAXIS III teacher assessment criteria research base*. Princeton, NJ: Educational Testing Service.

Kagan, D. M. (1990). Ways of evaluating teacher cognition: Inferences concerning the Goldilocks principle. *Review of Educational Research, 60*, 419-469.

Karweit, N. (1988). Time-on-task: The second time around. *NASSP Bulletin, 72*(505), 31-39.

Katz, L. G., & Raths, J. D. (1985). A framework for research on teacher education programs. *Journal of Teacher Education, 36*(6), 9-15.

Kauchak, D., & Peterson, K. (1987). *Teachers' thoughts on the assessment of their teaching*. Washington, DC: American Educational Research Association.

Keith, L., Tormatzky, L. G., & Pettigrew, L. E. (1974). An analysis of verbal and non-verbal classroom teaching behaviors. *Journal of Experimental Education, 42*(4), 30-38.

Kemessis, S. (1987). Critical reflection. In M. Wideen & I. Andrews (Eds.), *Staff development for school improvement* (pp. 73-90). Philadelphia: Falmer Press.

Klem, L. (1990, April). The challenge of understanding state content area requirements for the licensing of teachers. In C. Dwyer (Chair), *Defining the job of the beginning teacher: Multiple views*. Symposium conducted at the annual meeting of the American Educational Research Association, Boston.

Klem, L. (1992). *STAT state information tables, 1992*. Princeton, NJ: Educational Testing Service.

Klem, L. (1993a). *CHART*. Princeton, NJ: Educational Testing Service.

Klem, L. (1993b). *STAT*. Princeton, NJ: Educational Testing Service.

Klem, L. (1993c). *Project MATCH*. Princeton, NJ: Educational Testing Service.

Kochman, T. (1981). *Black and white styles in conflict*. Chicago: University of Chicago Press.

Krupczak, W. P. (1972). Relationships among student self-concept of academic ability, teacher perception of student academic ability and student achievement. (Doctoral Dissertation, University of Miami, 1972). *Dissertation Abstracts International, 33*, 3388A.

Kuligowski, B., Holdzkom, D., & French, R. L. (1993). Teacher performance evaluation in the southeastern states: Forms and functions. *Journal of Personnel Evaluation in Education, 6*, 335-358.

Leinhardt, G. (1992). What research on learning tells us about teaching. *Educational Leadership, 49*(7), 20-25.

Levin, H. M. (1987). Accelerated schools for disadvantaged students. *Educational Leadership, 44*(6), 19-21.

Little, J. W. (1992). *Teachers' professional development in a climate of educational reform.* Berkeley, CA: Consortium on Policy Research in Education.

Livingston, S. (1993). *Inter-assessor consistency of the PRAXIS III: Classroom Performance Assessments: Spring 1992 preliminary version.* Princeton, NJ: Educational Testing Service.

Logan, C. S., Garland, J. S., & Ellett, C. D. (1989). Large-scale teacher performance assessment instruments: A synthesis of what they measure and a national survey of their influence on the preparation of teachers. Paper presented at the annual meeting of the American Educational Research Association, San Francisco, CA.

Marzano, R. J., Brandt, R. S., Hughes, C. S., Jones, B. F., Presseisen, B. Z., Rankin, S. C., & Suhor, C. (1988). *Dimension of thinking: A framework for curriculum and instruction.* Alexandria, VA: Association for Supervision and Curriculum Development.

McCutcheon, G. (1980). How do elementary school teachers plan? The nature of planning and influences on it. In W. Doyle. & T. Good (Eds.), *Focus on teaching* (pp. 260-279). Chicago, IL: University of Chicago Press.

McDiarmid, G. W. (1991). What teachers need to know about cultural diversity: Restoring subject matter to the picture. In M. M. Kennedy (Ed.), *Teaching academic subjects to diverse learners* (pp. 257-269). New York: Teachers College Press.

McDonald, F. J. (Spring, 1976). Report on Phase II of the Beginning Teacher Evaluation study. *Journal of Teacher Education, 27*, 39-42.

Merwin, J. C. (1989). Evaluation. In M. C. Reynolds (Ed.), *Knowledge base for the beginning teacher* (pp. 185-192). New York: Pergamon.

Messick, S. (1992). Validity. In R. L. Linn (Ed.), *Educational Measurement* (3rd ed., pp.13-103). New York: Macmillan.

Michaels, S. (1981). Sharing time: Children's narrative styles and differential access to literacy. *Language in Society, 10,* 423-442.

Moll, L. C. (1988). Some key issues in teaching Latino students. *Language Arts, 65*(5), 465-472.

Moors, R. (1979). *Evaluating educational environments: Procedures, methods, findings and policy implications.* San Francisco, CA: Jossey-Bass.

Morine-Dershimer, G. (1977). *What's in a plan? Stated and unstated plans for lessons.* Sacramento, CA: California State Commission for Teacher Preparation and Licensing. (ERIC Document Reproduction Service No. ED 139 739).

Myford, C., Villegas, A. M., Reynolds, A., Camp, R., Jones, J., Knapp, J., Mandinach, E., Morris, L., & Sjostrom, B. (1993). *Formative studies of PRAXIS III: Classroom Performance Assessments, an overview.* Princeton, NJ: Educational Testing Service.

National Board for Professional Teaching Standards (1991). *Toward high and rigorous standards for the teaching profession* (3rd ed.). Detroit, MI: Author.

Natriello, G. (1987). *Evaluation processes in schools and classrooms* (Report No. 12). Baltimore, MD: Center for Social Organization of Schools. (ERIC Document Reproduction Service No. ED 294 890).

Nelson-Barber, S., & Meier, T. (1990). Multicultural context a key factor in teaching. *Academic Connections.* New York: The College Board.

Oakes, J. (1986). Tracking, inequity, and the rhetoric of school reform: Why schools don't change. *Journal of Education, 168* (1), 60-80.

Osborn, J., Jones, B., & Stein, M. (1985). The case for improving textbooks. *Educational Leadership, 42*(7), 9-16.

Paine, L. (1989). Orientation towards diversity: What do prospective teachers bring? (Research Report 89-9). East Lansing, MI: National Center for Research on Teacher Education.

Pajares, M. F. (1992). Teachers' beliefs and educational research: Cleaning up a messy act. *Review of Educational Research, 62,* 307-332.

Peterson, P. L., Marx, R. W., & Clark, C. M. (1978). Teacher planning, teacher behavior, and student achievement. *American Educational Research Journal, 15,* 417-432.

Pinnegar, S. (1989). *Teachers' knowledge of students and classrooms* Unpublished doctoral dissertation, University of Arizona, Tucson.

Porter, A. C., & Brophy, J. E. (1987, June). *Good teaching: Insights from the work of the Institute for Research on Teaching* (Occasional Paper No. 114). East Lansing, MI: The Institute for Research on Teaching, Michigan State University.

Porter, A., & Brophy, J. (1988). Synthesis of research on good teaching: Insights from the work of the Institute of Research on Teaching. *Educational Leadership, 45*(8), 74-85.

Powers, D. E. (1992). *Assessing the classroom performance of beginning teachers: Educators' appraisal of proposed evaluation criteria* (Research Report 92-56). Princeton, NJ: Educational Testing Service.

Powell, J. H., Casanova, U., & Berliner, D. C. (1991). *Parental involvement: Readings in educational research, a program for professional development, a National Education Association project.* Washington, DC: National Education Association.

Reynolds, A. (1992). What is competent beginning teaching? A review of the literature. *Review of Educational Research, 62*(1), 1-35.

Rist, R. (1970). Student social class and teacher expectations: The self-fulfilling prophecy in ghetto education. *Harvard Educational Review, 40*(3), 411-451.

Rodriguez, Y. E. G., Sjostrom, B. R., & Villegas, A. M. (1993). *Approaches to cultural diversity in the classroom: Implications for teacher education.* Paper presented at the annual meeting of the American Association of Colleges for Teacher Education, San Diego, CA.

Rosenfeld, M., Freeberg N. E., & Bukatko, P. (1992). *The professional functions of secondary school teachers* (Research Report 92-47). Princeton, NJ: Educational Testing Service.

Rosenfeld, M., Reynolds, A., & Bukatko, P. (1992). *The professional functions of elementary school teachers* (Research Report 92-53). Princeton, NJ: Educational Testing Service.

Rosenfeld, M., Wilder, G., & Bukatko, P. (1992). *The professional functions of middle school teachers* (Research Report 92-46). Princeton, NJ: Educational Testing Service.

Rosenshine, B. (1971). *Teaching behaviors and student achievement.* London: International Association for the Evaluation of Education.

Rosenshine, B. (1983). Teaching functions in instructional programs. *The Elementary School Journal, 83,* 335-353.

Rosenshine, B. (1987). Explicit teaching. In D. C. Berliner & B. V. Rosenshine (Eds.), *Talks to teachers* (pp. 75-92). New York: Random House.

Rosenshine, B., & Furst, N. (1971). Research on teacher performance criteria. In B. O. Smith (Ed.), *Research in Teacher Education* (pp.37-72). Englewood Cliffs, NJ: Prentice-Hall.

Rosenshine, B., & Stevens, R. (1986). Teaching functions. In M. C. Wittrock (Ed.), *Handbook of research on teaching* (3rd ed., pp. 376-391). New York: Macmillan.

Rosenthal, R. (1973). The Pygmalion effect lives. *Psychology Today, 7*(4), 56-60, 62-63.

Ross, J. A., & Regan, E. M. (1993). Sharing professional experience: Its impact on professional development. *Teaching and Teacher Education, 9*(1), 91-106.

Rutter, M., Maugham, B., Mortimore, P., Ouston, J., & Smith, A. (1979). *Fifteen thousand hours: Secondary schools and their effects on children.* Cambridge, MA: Harvard University Press.

Sanford. J. P., & Evertson, C. M. (1980). *Beginning the school year at a low SES junior high: Three case studies.* Austin, TX: The University of Texas at Austin, R&D Center for Teacher Education (ERIC Document Reproduction Service No. ED 195 547).

Schön, D. (1987). *Educating the reflective practitioner: Toward a new design for teaching and learning in the professions.* San Francisco: Jossey-Bass.

Schunk, D. H. (1991). Self-efficacy and academic motivation. *Educational Psychologist, 26,* 207-231.

Shulman, L. S. (1987). Knowledge and teaching: Foundations of the new reform. *Harvard Educational Review, 57*(1), 1-22.

Shulman, L. S. (1988a). A union of insufficiencies: Strategies for teacher assessment in a period of educational reform. *Educational Leadership, 46,* 36-41.

Shulman, L. S. (1988b). The paradox of teacher assessment. In *New directions for teacher assessment: Proceedings of the 1988 ETS Invitational Conference* (pp. 13-27). Princeton, NJ: Educational Testing Service.

Shulman, J. (1989). Blue freeways: Traveling the alternate route with big city teacher trainees. *Journal of Teacher Education, 40,* 2-8.

Sigel, I. E. (1990). What teachers need to know about human development. In D. D. Dill and Associates [sic], *What teachers need to know: The knowledge, skills, and values essential to good teaching* (pp. 76-93). San Francisco: Jossey-Bass.

Smith, L. R. (1985). A low-inference indicator of lesson organization. *Journal of Classroom Interaction, 21*(1), 25-30.

Smith, L. R., & Sanders, K. (1981). The effects of student achievement and student perception of varying structure in social studies content. *Journal of Educational Research, 74,* 333-336.

Smylie, M. (1988). The enhancement function of staff development: Organizational and psychological antecedents to individual teacher change. *American Educational Research Journal, 25,* 1-30.

Sparks-Langer, G. M., Simmons, J. M., Pasch, M., Colton, A. B., & Starko, A. (1990). Reflective pedagogical thinking: How can we promote it and measure it? *Journal of Teacher Education, 41*(4), 23-32.

Stage, E. (1989). *Strategies and materials for meeting the needs of all students in math, science, technology and health.* Sacramento, CA: California Curriculum Commission.

Stallings, J. A. (1982). Effective strategies for teaching basic skills. In I. Gordon (Ed.), *Developing Basic Skills Programs in Secondary Schools.* Alexandria, VA: Association for Supervision and Curriculum Development.

Stallings, J. A., & Kaskowitz, D. H. (1974). *Follow-through classroom evaluation, 1972-1993.* Menlo Park, CA: Stanford Research Institute (SRI) International.

Stein, M., & Wang, M. (1988). Teacher development and school improvement: The process of teacher change. *Teaching and Teacher Education, 4,* 171-187.

Sternberg, R. J., & Wagner, R. K. (1993). The g-centric view of intelligence and job performance is wrong. *Current Directions in Psychological Science, 2*(1), 1-4.

Stodolsky, S. S. (1988). *The subject matters.* Chicago: University of Chicago Press.

Street, M. S. (1991). *Content synthesis of currently used state-wide performance assessment instruments.* Princeton, NJ: Educational Testing Service.

Sykes, G., & Bird, T. (1992, August). Teacher education and the case idea. *Review of Research in Education, 18,* 457-521.

Taylor, A., & Valentine, B. (1985). *Effective schools. What research says about... series, No. 1, data-search reports.* Washington, DC: National Education Association. (ERIC Document Reproduction Service No. ED 274 073).

Tracy, S. J., & Smeaton, P. (1993). State-mandated assisting and assessing teachers: Levels of state control. *Journal of Personnel Evaluation in Education, 6,* 219-234.

U. S. Department of Education. (1987). *What works: Research about teaching and learning.* Washington, DC: U.S. Government Printing Office.

Van Patten, J., Chao, C., & Reigeluth, C. (1986). A review of strategies for sequencing and synthesizing instruction. *Review of Educational Research, 56*(4), 437-471.

Villegas, A. M. (1991). *Culturally responsive pedagogy for the 1990s and beyond.* Princeton, NJ: Educational Testing Service.

Villegas, A. M. (1992). *The competence needed by beginning teachers in a multicultural society.* Paper presented at the annual meeting of the American Association of Colleges of Teacher Education, San Antonio, TX.

Vosniadou, S. (1992). Knowledge acquisition and conceptual change. *Applied Psychology: An International Review, 41,* 347-357.

Walberg, H., Schiller, D., & Haertel, G. D. (1979). The great revolution in educational research. *Phi Delta Kappan, 61*(3), 179-182.

Walker, H. (1985). *Teacher social behavior standards and expectations as determinants of classroom ecology, teacher behavior, and child outcomes: Final Report.* Eugene, OR: Center for Educational Policy and Management, University of Oregon.

Weiss, J., & Louden, W. (1989). *Clarifying the notion of reflection.* Paper presented at the annual meeting of the American Educational Research Association, San Francisco.

Wesley, S., Rosenfeld, M., & Sims-Gunzenhauser, A. (1993). *Assessing the classroom performance of beginning teachers: Teachers' judgments of evaluation criteria.* Princeton, NJ: Educational Testing Service.

Wilkins, R. G. (1993). *PRAXIS III: Classroom Performance Assessments, collaborative fieldwork in Minnesota, March 1991-October 1992.* Princeton, NJ: Educational Testing Service.

Williams, P. S. (1988). Going west to get east: Using metaphors as instructional tools. *Journal of Children in Contemporary Society, 20*(1-2), 79-98.

Wittrock, M. C. (Ed.). (1985). *Handbook of research on teaching* (3rd ed.). New York: Macmillan.

Wong-Fillmore, L. W. (1990). *Now or later? Issues related to the early education of minority group students.* Washington, DC: Council of Chief State School Officers.

Woolfolk, A. E., & Hoy, W. K. (1990). Prospective teachers' sense of efficacy and beliefs about control. *Journal of Educational Psychology, 82,* 81-91.

Yinger, R. (1977). *A study of teacher planning: Description and theory development using ethnographic and information processing methods.* Unpublished doctoral dissertation, Michigan State University, East Lansing, MI.

Ysseldyke, J., Christenson, S., & Thurlow, M. L. (1987). *Instructional factors that influence student achievement: An integrative review* [Monograph No. 7]. Minneapolis, MN: University of Minnesota Instructional Alternatives Project.

Zahorik, J. A., (1975). Teachers' planning models. *Educational Leadership, 33,* 134-139.

Zeichner, K., & Tabachnick, B. R. (1991). Reflections on reflective teaching. In B. Tabachnick & K. Zeichner (Eds.), *Issues and practices in inquiry-oriented teacher education* (pp. 1-21). Philadelphia: Falmer Press.

Zigmond, N., Sansone, J., Miller, S., Donahoe, K., & Kohnke, R. (1986). Teaching learning disabled students at the secondary school level: What research says to teachers. *Learning Disabilities Focus, 1*(2), 108-115.

APPENDICES

A. Final (September, 1992) PRAXIS III: Classroom Performance Assessments Criteria, Descriptions, and Scoring Rules

B. PRAXIS III: Classroom Performance Assessments Instruments and Data Collection Forms

C. PRAXIS III: Classroom Performance Assessments Assessor Training Outline

D. Overview of the Assessment Process and Assessor Training for PRAXIS III: Classroom Performance Assessments

E. Three Developmental Versions of Criteria
    1. January 1992
    2. July 1991
    3. December 1990

F. List of Literature Review Panel Members
    1. Effective Teaching
    2. Teaching in Multicultural Classrooms

G. Members of National Advisory Committee for PRAXIS III: Classroom Performance Assessments

Appendix A

PRAXIS III: CLASSROOM PERFORMANCE ASSESSMENTS

ASSESSMENT CRITERIA

Domain A. *Organizing Content Knowledge for Student Learning*

Knowledge of the content to be taught underlies all aspects of good instruction. Domain A focuses on how teachers use their understanding of students and subject matter to decide on learning goals; to design or select appropriate activities and instructional materials; to sequence instruction in ways that will help students to meet short- and long-term curricular goals; and to design or select informative evaluation strategies. All of these processes, beginning with the learning goals, must be aligned with each other, and because of the diverse needs represented in any class, each of the processes mentioned must be carried out in ways that take into account the variety of knowledge and experiences that students bring to class. Therefore, knowledge of relevant information about the students themselves is an integral part of this domain.

Domain A is concerned with how the teacher thinks about the content to be taught. This thinking is evident in how the teacher organizes instruction for the benefit of her or his students.

The primary sources of evidence for the criteria in Domain A are the class profile, instruction profile, and preobservation interview. The classroom observation may also contribute to assessing performance on these criteria.

A1: Becoming familiar with relevant aspects of students' background knowledge and experiences

A2: Articulating clear learning goals for the lesson that are appropriate for the students

A3: Demonstrating an understanding of the connections between the content that was learned previously, the current content, and the content that remains to be learned in the future

A4: Creating or selecting teaching methods, learning activities, and instructional materials or other resources that are appropriate for the students and that are aligned with the goals of the lesson

A5: Creating or selecting evaluation strategies that are appropriate for the students and that are aligned with the goals of the lesson

A1 Becoming familiar with relevant aspects of students' background knowledge and experiences

Description

Research in cognitive science shows that students learn not simply by memorizing facts, but by reconfiguring and reorganizing what they already know. This means that students' experiences, both individual and cultural, are the essential material for learning. Teaching entails building bridges between the content to be learned and students' background knowledge and experiences. Therefore, teachers must become aware of these experiences.

Background knowledge and experiences include students' prior knowledge of the subject, their skills, interests, motivation to learn, developmental levels, and cultural experiences. Gaining information about some of these factors, such as prior knowledge or skills related to the content, may be relatively straightforward; for example, pretesting on the content to be taught can be a useful tool for the teacher. Less formal means, such as classroom discussion or observation of students, can contribute information not only about students' prior knowledge, but also about their interests, motivation, development levels, and cultural resources. Students as individuals differ with respect to any or all of these factors. Culturally, students differ in their beliefs, values, and ways of relating to the world. In classrooms, these cultural differences are manifested in how the students interact with each other and with the teacher, how they use language, how they approach learning tasks, and how they demonstrate what they know, among other things.

"Cultural differences" or "cultural diversity" are broadly defined to include ethnic differences, other differences associated with language group, socioeconomic background, and exceptionalities, as well as gender. To the extent possible, teachers should become familiar with and sensitive to the background experiences of students in these groups in order to build on students' experiences during instruction. However, group membership should never be used as a basis for stereotypical judgments about students.

Although teachers need knowledge of cultural differences, it would be unrealistic and impractical to expect beginning teachers to have a thorough understanding of the numerous cultural groups in our society. They should know, however, various procedures through which they can gain information about those communities that are represented in their classes. These procedures may include making home visits, conferring with community members, talking with parents, consulting with more-experienced colleagues, and observing children in and out of school to discern patterns of behavior that may be related to their cultural backgrounds.

The extent to which it is possible for teachers to become familiar with the various aspects of individual students' background knowledge and experiences may be affected by many factors, such as the number of students in the classroom and the amount of time each day that the teacher spends with a particular group. Teachers in self-contained classrooms, for example, may be expected to learn a great deal about their students' backgrounds and experiences. In some situations, such as a schedule and teaching load that assigns hundreds of students to one teacher, the teacher may be able to gain only a general understanding of the backgrounds of the students as a group. Regardless of their teaching assignment, however, all teachers need to know various procedures by which they can become familiar with their students' backgrounds and experiences.

As teachers gain skill, their understanding of the importance of gaining such information should deepen, and their knowledge of appropriate ways of gaining it should broaden.

Questions for Assessor Reflection

1. How does the teacher find out about students' background knowledge and experiences?

2. How does the teacher find out about students' foundation for understanding of the content?

3. Is the teacher able to describe why it is important to become familiar with students' background knowledge and experiences?

4. Is the teacher's degree of familiarity with students' background knowledge and experiences adequate in relation to the number of students he or she teaches?

A1 Scoring Rules

1.0 The teacher demonstrates a lack of understanding of why it is important to become familiar with students' background experiences, does not know how to find this information, and lacks familiarity with students' background experiences.

1.5 Above level 1.0, but below level 2.0

2.0 The teacher demonstrates some understanding of why it is important to become familiar with students' background experiences, describes one procedure used to obtain this information, and has some familiarity with the background knowledge and experiences of students in the class.

2.5 Above level 2.0, but below level 3.0

3.0 The teacher demonstrates a comprehensive understanding of why it is important to become familiar with students' background experiences, describes several procedures used to obtain this information, and demonstrates a clear understanding of students' background knowledge and experiences.

3.5 Above level 3.0

A2 Articulating clear learning goals for the lesson that are appropriate to the students

Description

A teacher should be able to translate the content of the lesson into goals for student learning. "Goals" should be understood to mean the desired learning outcomes or objectives for the lesson that will be observed. Goals may be expressed in various formats and terminology. It is critical, however, that goals—what the teacher wants the student to learn—be clearly distinguished from activities—what the teacher wants the students to do.

There are no restrictions to the kinds of learning that can be expressed in learning goals. In many cases, goals may refer to knowledge to be acquired—concepts, facts, and so on. In other situations, goals may address other kinds of learning; these may include, but are not limited to, values, thinking skills, social skills, performance skills, and behavioral goals. Regardless of the kind of goals involved, the teacher should be able to articulate how the students' actions, attitudes, knowledge, and/or skills will be modified or enhanced through their participation in the lesson.

At the basic level, this criterion asks teachers to translate their knowledge of content into goals that are stated as general learning outcomes. As the teacher gains skill, he or she should be able to support the goals by explaining why they are appropriate for this particular group of students and to modify or adjust expected outcomes to meet the needs of individual students in the class. If the teacher has no influence over the learning goals set for the class—for example, because of the specific requirements of a district-determined curriculum—the teacher should be able to explain how, and to what extent, the goals are appropriate for the whole class, or for groups or individual students within the class.

Questions for Assessor Reflection

1. Is the teacher able to state learning goals for the current lesson?

2. Does the teacher state the goals in terms of student outcomes, clearly distinguishing outcomes from activities?

3. Does the teacher give a clear rationale for the stated goals?

4. Does the teacher provide different goals for groups or individual students?

5. Does the teacher provide an acceptable explanation of why the differentiated goals are appropriate for groups or individual students?

A2 Scoring Rules

1.0 The teacher does not articulate clear learning goals

OR

the teacher has chosen goals that are inappropriate for the students.

1.5 Above level 1.0, but below level 2.0

2.0 The teacher articulates clear learning goals that are appropriate for the students.

2.5 Above level 2.0, but below level 3.0

3.0 The teacher articulates clear learning goals and provides a well-thought-out explanation of why they are appropriate for the students

OR

the teacher articulates clear learning goals that are appropriate to the students and are differentiated for groups or individual students in the class.

3.5 Above level 3.0

A3 Demonstrating an understanding of the connections between the content that was learned previously, the current content, and the content that remains to be learned in the future

Description

This criterion refers to a teacher's understanding of the structure or hierarchy of a discipline and of how knowing one element is prerequisite to or related to learning another. It contains two fundamental ideas. First, the teacher must be able to sequence content across lessons; she or he should be able to explain how the content of the lesson is related to what preceded it and how it is related to what will follow. Second, she or he should be able to draw on knowledge of the subject matter to explain where the current lesson fits within the broader scope of the discipline as a whole. That is, the teacher must be able to explain not only how the content of the lesson fits with what came before and what will follow, but also *why* this sequence is logical.

If the sequencing of content is outside the teacher's control, the teacher should still be able to identify and explain the connections, as well as the relationships, that this criterion addresses.

Questions for Assessor Reflection

1. Can the teacher explain how the content he or she has planned for today connects to what the students have previously learned?

2. Can the teacher explain how the content he or she has planned for today connects to what the students will study in the future?

3. To what extent can the teacher explain how today's lesson fits with larger goals of learning in the discipline?

A3 Scoring Rules

1.0 The teacher does not explain how the content of this lesson relates to the content of previous or future lessons

OR

the explanation given is illogical or inaccurate.

1.5 Above level 1.0, but below level 2.0

2.0 The teacher accurately explains how the content of this lesson relates to the content of previous or future lessons.

2.5 Above level 2.0, but below level 3.0

3.0 In addition to the requirements for level 2.0, the teacher accurately explains how the content of this lesson fits within the structure of the discipline.

3.5 Above level 3.0

A4 Creating or selecting teaching methods, learning activities, and instructional materials or other resources that are appropriate to the students and that are aligned with the goals of the lesson

Description

Instructional methods are the various ways in which teachers can structure learning activities. Methods are concerned with what teachers do; activities are concerned with what students do. Learning activities can involve students as a large group, in small groups, or individually. Activities should be designed to foster student involvement and to enhance the learning experience, whether the format is teacher presentation, teacher-led discussion, structured small-group work, peer teaching, programmed instruction, or some other format.

Activities range from teacher-directed through student-initiated. In deciding on teaching methods and selecting or designing learning activities, teachers should consider the learning goals and the preferred participation styles of students in the class. For example, some content is best conveyed through large-group discussion; other content lends itself better to small-group investigation. Similarly, some students may work better individually; others may benefit from cooperative group work. Whether the activities are created by the teacher or selected from those in a textbook or curriculum guide, the teacher should be able to provide a sound rationale for their use.

Instructional materials are concrete resources that students use to learn the content of the lesson. In some situations, no instructional materials are needed. If instructional materials are used, they may support any type of lesson. Materials need not be elaborate or expensive; for example, they may be "found" materials. Teachers should also be able to make use of relevant materials that students bring to class. In addition, the teacher may choose to draw on other resources, such as parents and community institutions. Whatever materials or resources are selected must be appropriate to the students. In a culturally or otherwise diverse classroom, this might require the use of a variety of types of materials.

Methods, activities, materials, and resources must be aligned with each other, and with the goals of the lesson. Activities, materials, and resources must all be developmentally appropriate for the students. At the basic level, this should be true for the students as a group. As teachers gain skill, they should be able to recognize the diverse needs of students and to meet those needs through the use of varied methods, activities and materials; the teacher's decisions should accommodate students in the class who have specific physical, emotional, behavioral or learning differences. For a given lesson, teachers should also gain skill at considering the various teaching methods, activities, materials, and resources, and selecting or creating those that will best meet students' needs.

Questions for Assessor Reflection

1. Are the methods, activities, materials, and resources selected by the teacher aligned with the goals of the lesson?

2. Are the methods and activities appropriate to the students' developmental levels? Do the materials and activities provide for varied styles of participation?

3. Are the activities, materials, and resources appropriate to the students' developmental levels? Do they reflect the common and unique experiences of different ethnic groups, of males and females, of different economic groups, of groups with exceptionalities? Are the activities, and resources appropriate for students of limited English proficiency?

4. If a single activity is used, can the teacher provide a sound explanation of why a single activity is appropriate for all students?

5. Is there evidence that the teacher has considered various methods, activities, and materials, and has considered the advantages and disadvantages of each?

A4 Scoring Rules

1.0 The teacher chooses methods, activities, or materials* that are unrelated to the goals of the lesson

OR

the methods, activities, or materials* are clearly not appropriate to the students.

1.5 Above level 1.0, but below level 2.0

2.0 The teacher chooses methods, activities, and materials* that are aligned with the goals of the lesson and that are appropriate to the students in general.

2.5 Above level 2.0, but below level 3.0

3.0 In addition to the requirements for level 2.0, the teacher chooses methods, activities, and materials* that allow a differentiated learning experience for individuals or groups of students

OR

the teacher provides a sound explanation of why the single teaching method or learning activity in the lesson is appropriate for all students.

3.5 Above level 3.0

* "Materials" includes all resources that the teacher might use. If the lesson requires no materials, there is no penalty to the teacher for not using them.

A5 Creating or selecting evaluation strategies that are appropriate for the students and that are aligned with the goals of the lesson

Description

It is only through well-designed evaluation strategies that a teacher knows whether students have achieved the learning goals for the lesson and is able to plan further learning experiences. Evaluation strategies must be aligned with, and reflect, the goals of the lesson. If the goals relate to *individual* student learning, then the plan for evaluation should do so, too; if the goals relate to *small- or large-group* outcomes, as in a performing music group, then the plan for evaluation should also do so.

A plan for evaluation of student learning may include one or more formats. The teacher may create evaluation strategies (for example, teacher-made tests or student portfolios) or select them from the instructional materials used (for example, the chapter test from a textbook). For certain types of goals, tests may be less appropriate than other strategies, such as observation of student performance. Many teachers involve students in self-evaluation or peer evaluation. Whatever the strategy, evaluation must be systematic. That is, it must provide the teacher with useful information about the extent to which the instructional goals—whether individual or group—have been met. As the teacher gains experience, she or he will gain understanding of how the results of the evaluation can be used to help in planning future instruction.

Evaluation strategies must be appropriate for the students. Since the goal of evaluation is to gather information about learning, the strategies chosen should provide students with clear opportunities to demonstrate their learning. In culturally diverse classrooms, student evaluation is especially complex. Children from different groups may enter school with culturally specific understandings of the appropriate ways of displaying knowledge. If the teacher and students do not share these understandings, the teacher may misjudge the students' competence unless he or she is sensitive to these cultural differences. Because reliance on a single form of evaluation may place some students at a disadvantage, teachers may need to use a variety of strategies to evaluate student learning. This is especially relevant for students of limited English proficiency and for many students with exceptionalities.

Evaluation strategies may be implemented at a time later than the observed lesson. While some monitoring of student learning occurs in class on a daily basis, most systematic evaluation is separated in time from instruction. The nature of the lesson and the unit will determine not only the form, but also the timing of evaluation. In many cases, evaluation of the lesson being assessed may be part of the evaluation of a longer unit of instruction.

A critical element of this criterion is that the strategy or plan is designed to provide information about how well the learning goals of this lesson have been met. In most cases, the assessor will *not* see the evaluation strategies being implemented; however, the teacher must provide oral or written evidence of a plan for the evaluation of learning goals.

Questions for Assessor Reflection

1. How is the plan for evaluation aligned with the learning goals of the lesson?

2. Is the plan for evaluation sufficiently systematic to provide the teacher with useful information about the extent to which learning goals have been met?

3. Is the evaluation appropriate to the students in the class? What methods are used? How are students of limited English proficiency and students with exceptionalities provided with opportunities to display their knowledge of content?

4. Can the teacher describe how he or she will use the results of the evaluation in planning future instruction?

A5 Scoring Rules

1.0 The teacher has not provided for systematically evaluating student learning

OR

the evaluation planned is clearly inappropriate either to the goals of the lesson or to the students.

1.5 Above level 1.0, but below level 2.0

2.0 The teacher has a plan for systematically evaluating student learning that is aligned with the goals of the lesson and appropriate to the students.

2.5 Above level 2.0, but below level 3.0

3.0 In addition to the requirements for level 2.0, the teacher can describe how he or she will use the results of the evaluation in planning future instruction.

3.5 Above level 3.0

Domain B: *Creating an Environment for Student Learning*

Domain B relates to the social and emotional components of learning as prerequisites to academic achievement. Thus, most of the criteria in this domain focus on the human interactions in the classroom, on the connections between teachers and students, and among students. Domain B addresses issues of fairness and rapport, of helping students to believe that they can learn and can meet challenges, of establishing and maintaining constructive standards for behavior in the classroom. It also includes the learning "environment" in the most literal sense — the physical setting in which teaching and learning take place.

A learning environment that provides both emotional and physical safety for students is one in which a broad range of teaching and learning experiences can occur. Teachers must be able to use their knowledge of their students in order to interpret their students' behavior accurately and respond in ways that are appropriate and supportive. When they do so, their interactions with students consistently foster the students' sense of self-esteem. In addition, teachers' efforts to establish a sense of the classroom as a community with clear standards should never be arbitrary; all behavioral standards and teacher-student interactions should be grounded in a sense of respect for students as individuals.

Evidence for the criteria in Domain B will be drawn primarily from the classroom observation; supporting evidence may be drawn from both the pre- and postobservation interviews. The class profile provides contextual information relevant to these criteria.

B1: Creating a climate that promotes fairness

B2: Establishing and maintaining rapport with students

B3: Communicating challenging learning expectations to each student

B4: Establishing and maintaining consistent standards of classroom behavior

B5: Making the physical environment as safe and conducive to learning as possible

B1 Creating a climate that promotes fairness

Description

This criterion is concerned with the teacher's ability to facilitate and maintain fair classroom interactions between the teacher and the students and among students. "Fairness" here means helping all students to have access to learning and to feel that they are equally valued in the classroom. In this sense, promoting fairness also implies promoting a sense of self-worth for each student. The teacher should consistently provide good examples of fairness. At the same time, fair treatment should *not* be interpreted to mean a formulaic, rigid, or stereotype-based way of "treating all students the same."

The teacher must be fair in the treatment of students of different genders, ethnicity, cultural backgrounds, and socioeconomic levels, as well as those with exceptionalities. The teacher should be familiar with and value the diverse ways in which students express themselves and interact with one another. Examples of unfair teacher behavior include giving praise to high achievers only, "playing favorites," allowing particular individuals or groups of students to be consistently off-task without trying to reengage them in the activity, asking or allowing only some students to respond to questions, making comments about students that are demeaning, and stereotyping. In contrast, to create a climate that promotes fairness, the teacher should convey and act on the attitude that all students are important, and that they all have a right to learning opportunities and attention. The teacher should not accept without a response comments and interactions by students with each other or with the teacher that are demeaning, based on stereotypes, or otherwise unfair.

As the teacher gains skill, she or he should be able to help students develop a sense of fairness—what it means and how it takes shape—in their interactions with each other.

Questions for Assessor Reflection

1. Is the teacher fair in interactions with students during the observed class period?

2. In what ways does the teacher help students to have access to learning?

3. In what ways does the teacher help the students feel equally valued in the classroom?

4. Are there patterns of either exclusion or overattention in student-teacher interactions?

5. Does the teacher show evidence of stereotyped views of students?

6. Is the teacher inappropriately negative in remarks to students?

7. Do students treat each other fairly?

8. Does the teacher respond appropriately to stereotype-based, demeaning, or other unfair comments by students?

B1 Scoring Rules

1.0 The teacher is unfair in the treatment of students

OR

the teacher tolerates obviously unfair behavior among students.

1.5 Above level 1.0, but below level 2.0

2.0 The teacher is fair in the treatment of students and does not accept obviously unfair behavior among students.

2.5 Above level 2.0, but below level 3.0

3.0 The teacher is fair in the treatment of students and actively encourages fairness among students.

3.5 Above level 3.0

B2 Establishing and maintaining rapport with students

Description

This criterion is concerned with the teacher's ability to relate positively to students as people. The teacher might demonstrate traits such as genuine concern, warmth, sincerity, and humor. Additional ways of establishing rapport include exhibiting interest in students as unique individuals, acknowledging the traditions and customs of students with differing ethnic backgrounds, and taking time to listen to students. Effective interpersonal and communication skills also contribute to establishing rapport. Comments that indicate, either directly or indirectly, an understanding of students' lives outside of school also provide evidence of rapport. Other indicators of rapport can include making eye contact, smiling, making focused comments or a friendly joke, maintaining appropriate proximity to students, and so on.

Rapport can appear in a wide range of forms. Students' developmental levels will have a significant impact on what constitutes appropriate attempts to establish rapport. For example, some kinds of physical contact may be appropriate with young children, but inappropriate with older students. In addition, teachers, like students, are diverse; there is no single "right way" to achieve rapport. Because teacher-student rapport can be manifested in so many different ways, the assessor must be careful to consider rapport in specific rather than general terms; is the teacher's attempt to establish or maintain rapport appropriate, given the context in which the teacher is working? For example, a comment by a teacher might be interpreted as undesirably sarcastic in one context, but as supportive in another. In such a situation, the assessor must consider the students' reactions, or ask about the interaction in the post-observation interview.

As the teacher gains skill, he or she should be able to build on a basis of understanding students and should have a better sense of what is appropriate and likely to work with students.

Questions for Assessor Reflection

1. Does the teacher attempt to relate positively to students?

2. Does the teacher show concern for the students?

3. Does the teacher tailor personal interactions according to the individual characteristics of students?

4. Do the teacher's attempts to establish rapport take into account the students' backgrounds and experiences?

5. Are the teacher's attempts to establish rapport appropriate to the students' developmental levels?

B2 Scoring Rules

1.0 The teacher does not attempt to establish rapport with students

OR

the teacher's attempts are inappropriate.

1.5 Above level 1.0, but below level 2.0

2.0 The teacher establishes a basic level of rapport with the students.

2.5 Above level 2.0, but below level 3.0

3.0 The teacher successfully establishes rapport in ways that are appropriate to students' diverse backgrounds and needs.

3.5 Above level 3.0

B3 Communicating challenging learning expectations to each student

Description

The teacher must convey the attitude that school is a place for learning and that *all* students can learn. The teacher should communicate explicitly or implicitly a belief that each student is capable of significant achievement. For example, the teacher might select learning goals that are rigorous or challenging for the students, but within their reach, and combine this with encouragement for students to have confidence, to take risks, and in general to strive for success.

Given the likelihood that students in the class will have varying levels of skills, abilities, and achievements, the challenging expectations for each student may—in absolute terms—be somewhat different. A reciprocal relationship frequently exists between expectations and performance. Other things being equal, students may put forth more effort, with greater energy, if they believe that their teacher anticipates that they will perform well. As a result of this effort and energy, students' work frequently meets a high standard, enhancing the students' capabilities in the eyes of the teacher, and encouraging the teacher to hold high standards for future work.

This criterion includes two distinct, though related, ideas. First, a teacher's confidence in students can help them "stretch," tackling challenging tasks or understanding difficult concepts. Second, a teacher's high standards for students can encourage them to produce work of high quality, completed with conscientious attention, that becomes a source of pride for the students. As the teacher gains skill, he or she should be able to draw on familiarity with students' background knowledge and experiences to communicate challenging expectations that are suitable for individual students or groups of students.

Questions for Assessor Reflection

1. How does the teacher show, by words, actions, or attitude, that each student is capable of meaningful achievement?

2. In what ways do the students demonstrate a clear understanding of the teacher's expectations for achievement that may have been stated explicitly prior to the observation?

3. Are the learning expectations for students challenging but within their reach?

B3 Scoring Rules

1.0 The teacher communicates explicitly or implicitly to individuals, to groups within the class, or to the class as a whole that they are incapable of learning or that the teacher's expectations for their learning are very low.

1.5 Above level 1.0, but below level 2.0

2.0 The teacher does nothing to communicate to any student that he or she is incapable of meeting learning expectations.

2.5 Above level 2.0, but below level 3.0

3.0 The teacher actively encourages students to meet challenging learning expectations.

3.5 Above level 3.0

B4 Establishing and maintaining consistent standards of classroom behavior

Description

This criterion refers to the desired standards of teacher and student inter-action that will ensure an appropriate climate for learning. Both students and teacher may contribute to the development of standards for appropriate classroom behavior. The exact nature of such standards may vary widely, in response to students' developmental levels, their cultural backgrounds, the subject being taught, the model of teaching that is implemented, the level of noise or informality that the teacher is comfortable with, and so on. Once established and agreed on, these standards must be maintained consistently, although there will of course be situations that require "exceptions to the rule."

It is not expected that all students will behave at all times in accordance with the behavioral standards for the class. Students as individuals obviously differ widely in their attitudes and their willingness to accept behavioral standards; in addition, classes, as groups, have their own "personalities." In all cases, it is important for the teacher both to demonstrate positive behavior and to make sure that students understand the consequences for breaches of the agreed-on standards of behavior. At the basic level, teachers may have trouble anticipating potentially disruptive behavior and may, therefore, have to respond frequently to major disruptions (that is, behavior that constitutes a serious breach of the standards for the class). As the teacher gains skill she or he should be able to move to a level of skill that enables her or him to handle the range of behavior issues more consistently and effectively and to anticipate misbehavior.

The assessor should not expect to see the teacher actively establishing standards for behavior during every lesson that is observed; in many cases, the students' behavior may enable the assessor to infer that standards have been established and maintained. In evaluating how standards of behavior have been established, implemented, and maintained, it is also important to keep in mind that there is a range of standards for behavior that can contribute to a range of positive learning environments. There is no single right way to keep order. In all cases, however, the standards must embody a sense of respect for students as people.

If there are school policies that affect standards of classroom behavior, the assessor should be aware of them and of the rationale for them.

Questions for Assessor Reflection

1. Are consistent standards of classroom behavior evident?

2. How are standards established?

3. Does the teacher model respectful and appropriate standards of behavior?

4. Do established standards of behavior convey a sense of respect for the students?

5. How are the standards maintained?

6. How does the teacher respond to serious behavior problems? Are her or his responses appropriate?

7. Does the teacher respond to inappropriate behavior consistently and appropriately?

B4 Scoring Rules

1.0 The teacher makes no attempt to respond to disruptive behavior

OR

the teacher's response to disruptive behavior does not demonstrate respect for the students.

1.5 Above level 1.0, but below level 2.0

2.0 The teacher makes appropriate attempts to respond to disruptive behavior in ways that demonstrate respect for the students

OR

there is no disruptive behavior during the lesson.

2.5 Above level 2.0, but below level 3.0

3.0 In addition to the requirements for level 2.0, the teacher responds to minor misbehavior consistently and with reasonable success, in ways that demonstrate respect for students

OR

student behavior during the lesson is consistently appropriate.

3.5 Above level 3.0

B5 Making the physical environment as safe and conducive to learning as possible

Description

This criterion focuses on the physical setting in which learning is to take place—the degree of harmony or match between the arrangement of the physical environment and the planned lesson or activity. Student safety and students' diverse physical needs also fall within the realm of this criterion.

In assessing this criterion, it is essential to consider the degree of control that the teacher has over the physical environment. For example, if the furniture is securely anchored to the floor or if the teacher moves from classroom to classroom, serious limitations are placed on the teacher's opportunities to demonstrate effective use of space.

When the teacher does have control of the learning space, the assessor's attention should focus on the effect that the physical arrangements have on learning. In some situations, such as lab sciences, vocational education, or home economics, it is especially important for the arrangement to reflect a concern for students' safety. In addition, the room should be organized so that all students, including those with special needs, have access to instruction. If the teacher has no control over the physical environment, attention should be given to how the teacher adjusts the lesson or activity to the setting, despite this drawback. As the teacher gains skill he or she is able to use the physical space as a resource that facilitates learning—that is, the physical space becomes an element that contributes to the effectiveness of instruction. For example, a French or ESL teacher might label the door, windows, shelves, and other objects in the classroom in the language being taught. In a primary-grade classroom, the teacher might take care to position bulletin-board displays and other visual materials at the children's eye level.

Another factor to consider in this criterion is the affective dimension of the physical setting. The presence or absence of displays of student work, the level of diversity evident in displays, the attractiveness of the space, and the degree of overall appeal as a place for learning are variables in this aspect of the criterion. Though such characteristics may be highly variable according to context and relatively difficult to judge, they are part of the decision concerning "conducive to learning" included here.

Questions for Assessor Reflection

1. How much control does the teacher have over the physical environment?

2. Are any safety violations or risks evident?

3. To what extent is there a match between the lesson or activity and the furniture or room configuration?

4. Is the space arranged so that all students, including those with special needs, have access to the lesson?

5. How does the room reflect the learning that takes place there?

B5 Scoring Rules

1.0 The teacher allows the physical environment to be unsafe

OR

the teacher allows the physical environment to interfere with learning.

1.5 Above level 1.0, but below level 2.0

2.0 The teacher creates a physical environment that is safe and does not interfere with learning.

2.5 Above level 2.0, but below level 3.0

3.0 The teacher uses the physical environment as a resource to facilitate learning. Provisions are made to accommodate all students, including those with special needs. If the teacher does not control the physical environment, he or she effectively adjusts the activities to the existing physical environment.

3.5 Above level 3.0

Domain C: *Teaching for student learning*

This domain focuses on the act of teaching and its overall goal: helping students to connect with the content. As used here, "content" refers to the subject matter of a discipline and may include knowledge, skills, perceptions and values in any domain: cognitive, social, artistic, physical and so on. Teachers direct students in the process of establishing individual connections with the content, thereby devising a good "fit" for the content within the framework of the students' knowledge, interests, abilities, cultural backgrounds and personal backgrounds. At the same time, teachers should help students to move beyond the limits of their current knowledge or understanding. Teachers monitor learning, making certain that students assimilate information accurately and that they understand and can apply what they have learned. Teachers must also be sure that students understand what is expected of them procedurally during the lesson and that class time is used to good purpose.

Most of the evidence for a teacher's performance with respect to these criteria will come from the classroom observation. It may be augmented or illuminated by evidence from the pre and postobservation interviews.

C1: Making learning goals and instructional procedures clear to students

C2: Making content comprehensible to students

C3: Encouraging students to extend their thinking

C4: Monitoring students' understanding of content through a variety of means, providing feedback to students to assist learning, and adjusting learning activities as the situation demands

C5: Using instructional time effectively

C1 Making learning goals and instructional procedures clear to students

Description

This criterion relates to clear communication of both the learning goals for the specific lesson and the instructional procedures that will be used to attain these goals. There are many ways of communicating learning goals to the students. Sometimes the teacher will make the learning goals explicit for the students at the beginning of the lesson, either orally or in writing. This explicit approach is usually used in direct instruction. At other times, the teacher will wait until the end of the lesson, then help the students to infer the learning goals. This implicit approach is often used in inquiry or discovery lessons. Regardless of the instructional strategy used by the teacher, whether direct or indirect, the students should understand that instruction is purposeful.

Students also need to understand the instructional procedures for the lesson—that is, how they are expected to participate in learning activities. Teachers can communicate instructional procedures in a variety of ways that may include, but are not limited to, oral or written directions, explanations or review of the tasks at hand, written contracts with individual students. All instructions or directions given to students about learning activities should be clear, regardless of the specific focus—e.g., completing a worksheet, performing a complex experiment, creating a work of art, cooperating in a group project. In addition, if an out-of-class assignment is given to students, the procedures for carrying out the assignment should be clear.

As the teacher gains experience, he or she should communicate to students, either implicitly or explicitly, how the instructional procedures for the lesson are related to the learning goals.

Questions for Assessor Reflection

1. Does the teacher communicate learning goals to the students, either explicitly or implicitly?

2. Are the directions to students for instructional procedures clear?

3. How does the teacher help students of different backgrounds (ethnic groups, language groups, males and females, students with exceptionalities) understand the learning goals of the lesson?

4. How does the teacher help students of different backgrounds (ethnic groups, language groups, males and females, students with exceptionalities) understand the instructional procedures used in the lesson?

5. Are the students able to carry out the instructional procedures?

C1 Scoring Rules

1.0 **The teacher provides the students with no information, confusing information, or inaccurate information about the learning goals or the instructional procedures for the lesson.**

1.5 Above level 1.0, but below level 2.0

2.0 **The students receive accurate information about the learning goals. The teacher provides the students with clear, accurate information about the instructional procedures for the lesson, and most of the students seem to understand.**

2.5 Above level 2.0, but below level 3.0

3.0 **In addition to the requirements for Level 2.0, the students seem to understand the learning goals fully. The teacher ensures that all students, including those who may initially have trouble, understand and can carry out the instructional procedures for the lesson.**

3.5 Above level 3.0

C2 Making content comprehensible to students

Description

This criterion focuses on how the teacher's understanding and organization of content—central issues of Domain A—come to life in the classroom. When the teacher is able to make an effective transition from thinking about content to involving students with it, the content is comprehensible to students; that is, students are able to learn by connecting the new content being taught with what is already familiar to them.

In order to learn, students must be engaged with the content and the content must be meaningful to them on some level, whether that level is deeply personal or more purely academic. Therefore, one aspect of this criterion is the teacher's skill at activating and building on students' background knowledge and experiences in order to make the content meaningful to them. The content being taught and the particular situation will, of course, influence how the teacher goes about this. For example, reviews of the content may help students to activate relevant knowledge. Questions or discussions that draw on students' experiences outside of school may enable them to draw on less-academic knowledge that will help them to become engaged with and understand the content of the lesson. Such strategies provide opportunities to help students of diverse background or needs make connections with the content and become engaged with learning. Because student engagement is *not* likely to occur if the content is incomprehensible, engagement can, in many situations, serve as sound evidence that the students understand the content. However, it is essential to recognize that engagement should involve genuine processing of content, not merely looking busy or becoming involved in activities that are irrelevant to the learning goals.

The teacher should be able to organize instruction through a variety of approaches, such as presentations, small-group or individual work, and student-initiated projects. Such approaches may be used in direct instruction by the teacher or be incorporated into lessons in which students have more control over the learning environment. When the teacher is communicating content directly, it must be clear and accurate and the teacher should use his or her content knowledge in developing explanations, descriptions, examples, analogies, metaphors, demonstrations, discussions, and learning activities that build bridges to the students' background knowledge and experience. If the teacher uses a relatively nondirective approach (e.g., an inquiry lesson) that allows the students more control over the learning experience, the process or structure of the lesson should itself contribute to making content comprehensible.

As teachers gain skill, they should be able to structure a lesson in such a way that it is understood not only as a series of discrete pieces of information, but as a group or series of interrelated ideas or processes. For this to occur, the structure of the lesson itself must be coherent; that is, the parts of the lesson must be sequenced logically, so that students can readily follow the lesson's progression. The order of activities makes sense conceptually, and the lesson seems to flow. When a lesson is coherent, its structure actually helps students to understand the content.

Questions for Assessor Reflection

1. Does the teacher communicate content clearly and accurately? Is this done equitably for females and males, students of different ethnic groups, students of different economic groups, students with exceptionalities, students of limited English proficiency?

2. In lessons that are not teacher-directed, has the teacher structured the learning environment or process in a way that enables students to understand the content?

3. Are students generally engaged with the content?

4. Does the lesson as a whole have a coherent structure?

C2 Scoring Rules

1.0 The content appears to be incomprehensible to the students

OR

the lesson contains substantive inaccuracies.

1.5 Above level 1.0, but below level 2.0

2.0 The content is accurate and appears to be comprehensible to the students.

2.5 Above level 2.0, but below level 3.0

3.0 In addition to the requirements for Level 2.0, the lesson as a whole has a logical and coherent structure.

3.5 Above level 3.0

C3 Encouraging students to extend their thinking

Description

This criterion focuses on the aspects of teaching in *any* situation that encourage students to develop and have confidence in their own ability to think independently, creatively, or critically. The term "thinking" is used broadly here, and "extending their thinking" does not necessarily imply elaborate exercises, or activities that are foreign to the subject being taught.

Sometimes students do learn content through simple, low-level cognitive processes, for example, by memorizing vocabulary in other languages or procedures for a mathematical operation. More frequently, however, teachers enable students to move beyond the "facts" and extend their thinking, for example, by having them make connections between different events, predict the outcome of a story, or invent another method of solving a problem.

Teachers use many instructional techniques to encourage students to extend their thinking—for example, asking open-ended questions, allowing students adequate time to think about their answers to questions, or assigning tasks in which there is more than one method of completing the task. Through all these strategies, the teacher invites students to extend their thinking.

Nontraditional subject areas also provide opportunities for extending thinking. Solving problems creatively requires thinking, whether the subject area is science, visual art, home economics, shop, or any other area. When the content being studied involves primarily physical skills, extending thinking may become a matter of helping students to recognize the possibilities inherent in skills learned, to integrate skills, or to consider the strategic possibilities in their choice of skills. Similarly, in performance classes, such as drama, extending thinking may involve helping students to integrate performance skills or to understand the relationships between skills or techniques and the performance as a whole.

Many opportunities for students to extend their thinking arise spontaneously in teaching, as when the teacher asks students for their opinions or for alternative explanations. As teachers gain skill, they frequently design an activity or a lesson specifically to encourage students to extend their thinking, as when students are asked to write an essay comparing one author to another, or to consider questions such as why leaves turn brown in the fall, or to offer constructive criticisms of their own or each other's work or performance.

Questions for Assessor Reflection

1. Does the teacher recognize and use opportunities to help students extend their thinking?

2. Is the teacher able to use the current content appropriately as a springboard to independent, creative, or critical thinking?

3. Does the teacher challenge students' thinking in ways relevant to their background knowledge and experiences?

4. Does the teacher structure specific learning activities that encourage students to extend their thinking?

C3 Scoring Rules

1.0 **The teacher discourages students from thinking independently, creatively, or critically.**

1.5 Above level 1.0, but below level 2.0

2.0 **The teacher encourages students to think independently, creatively, or critically in the context of the content being studied.**

2.5 Above level 2.0, but below level 3.0

3.0 **The teacher uses activities or strategies that are specifically designed to actively encourage students to think independently, creatively, or critically about the content being taught.**

3.5 Above level 3.0

C4 Monitoring students' understanding of content through a variety of means, providing feedback to students to assist learning, and adjusting learning activities as the situation demands

Description

This criterion refers to the monitoring, feedback, and adjustment that takes place *during the lesson*. The teacher should monitor the students' understanding of the content throughout the lesson. Monitoring may be accomplished by a variety of means—checking written work, asking questions, paying attention to nonverbal cues from students, and so on. In some specialized situations (e.g., large choir rehearsal), it may be appropriate to monitor groups (e.g., altos) rather than individual students.

In a culturally diverse classroom, especially one that includes students of limited English proficiency, the teacher must be especially sensitive to the verbal and nonverbal signals that each student might use to indicate that he or she is confused or does not understand what is expected. This may require insight into culturally specific ways of expressing understanding and confusion. For example, silence may denote comprehension in one group, but confusion in another.

The teacher should provide specific feedback to reinforce those who are on track and redirect or assist those who need extra help. Feedback can take the form of specific comments to individuals or remarks to groups of students, or it can be nonverbal. Depending how instruction is organized, feedback can come from sources other than the teacher, such as other students, books, self-checking materials, or the activity itself.

The teacher should use information gained from monitoring students' understanding to assess the effectiveness of the particular instructional approach. As the teacher gains skill, he or she should be able to adjust the learning activities as necessary if they are not working as intended or if the students are having unexpected problems. In addition, the teacher may choose to adjust instruction not because of problems, but because he or she recognizes a "teachable moment" and adjusts instruction in order to capitalize on it.

Monitoring, feedback, and adjustment must take into account all of the students in the class. If a group of students is consistently disregarded, or if a group receives the majority of the teacher's attention and the teacher can give no sound reason for this, then monitoring, feedback, and adjustment are not adequate. In some cases monitoring may be difficult to observe directly; in such cases feedback to students or adjustment of the lesson can serve as evidence that monitoring has occurred.

Questions for Assessor Reflection

1. Does the teacher monitor students' understanding of the content? Is this done equitably?

2. Does the teacher provide substantive feedback to students? Is this done equitably?

3. Does the teacher adjust learning activities as needed? Is the adjustment equitable?

C4 Scoring Rules

1.0 The teacher makes no attempt to determine whether students are understanding and gives them no feedback.

1.5 Above level 1.0, but below level 2.0

2.0 The teacher monitors the students' understanding of the content. The students receive feedback as necessary.

2.5 Above level 2.0, but below level 3.0

3.0 The teacher monitors individual students' or groups of students' understanding of the content and makes appropriate instructional adjustments if necessary. If appropriate, students receive substantive and specific feedback.

3.5 Above level 3.0

C5 Using instructional time effectively

Description

This criterion refers to the teacher's skill in using time effectively during the lesson. As used here, "instructional" time means time during which content-related teaching and learning take place. "Noninstructional" time, on the other hand, is time spent on activities that are a necessary part of classroom life, but don't contribute to learning.

An important aspect of using time effectively, is pacing the lesson in ways that are appropriate to the students in the class. In well-paced instruction, the amount of time spent on learning activities is appropriate to the content, the learners, and the situation. If the pace of instruction is too fast, some or all of the students may not be able to understand the content being taught. When lessons are paced too slowly, students may become bored and student engagement may decline. Digressions from the planned activities do not constitute a waste of time if they result in valuable learning; digressions that simply wander into irrelevant topics for substantial periods of time should be avoided. If a lesson or learning activity is completed more quickly than the teacher anticipated, he or she should provide the students with meaningful and relevant work or activities for the remaining instructional time.

Using time effectively also implies making sure that time spent on necessary but *noninstructional* processes is minimized. Therefore, effective classroom routines and procedures for such noninstructional processes as taking roll and distributing materials contribute positive evidence for this criterion, since they enable the teacher to spend more class time on learning activities. As the teacher gains skill, her or his sense of appropriate pacing should become more accurate, and the efficiency with which noninstructional routines are conducted should increase. Time should *not* be considered wasted if the reasons for the problem (for example, a lengthy interruption via a PA system) are outside the teacher's control.

142

Questions for Assessor Reflection

1. Is the instruction paced in such a way that students appear to be on task most of the time?

2. Is there evidence of established routines and procedures that help the teacher maximize the time available for instruction?

3. If a noninstructional interruption occurs, is instruction resumed efficiently?

4. Do all students have meaningful work or activities for the entire instructional time?

C5 Scoring Rules

1.0 Substantial amounts of instructional time are spent on activities of little instructional value

OR

the pacing of the lesson is inappropriate to the content and/or the students.

1.5 Above level 1.0, but below level 2.0

2.0 The pacing of the lesson is appropriate for most of the students. Noninstructional procedural matters do not occupy an excessive amount of time.

2.5 Above level 2.0, but below level 3.0

3.0 The teacher provides students with activities of instructional value for the entire instructional time and paces them appropriately. Any necessary noninstructional procedures are performed efficiently.

3.5 Above level 3.0

Domain D: *Teacher Professionalism*

Teachers must be able to evaluate their own instructional effectiveness in order to plan specific future lessons for particular classes and to improve their teaching over time. They should be able to discuss the degree to which different aspects of a lesson were successful in terms of instructional approaches, student responses, and learning outcomes. Teachers should be able to explain how they will proceed to work toward learning for *all* students. The professional responsibilities of all teachers, including beginning teachers, also include sharing appropriate information with other professionals and with families in ways that support the learning of diverse student populations.

The primary source of evidence for the criteria in Domain D is the postobservation interview.

D1: Reflecting on the extent to which the learning goals were met

D2: Demonstrating a sense of efficacy

D3: Building professional relationships with colleagues to share teaching insights and to coordinate learning activities for students

D4: Communicating with parents or guardians about student learning

D1 Reflecting on the extent to which the learning goals were met

Description

Teaching extends far beyond interaction with students in the classroom, and includes reflection both before and after classroom instruction. Teachers must be able to reflect on classroom events, both in order to plan next steps for individuals or groups of students and in order to improve their teaching skills over time. Toward these ends, this criterion focuses on the teacher's skill in determining the extent to which the students in the class achieved the learning goals. In order to plan the next lessons for this group of students, the teacher must know the extent to which individuals and groups of students achieved the goals for this lesson. For example, if a certain group did not understand a concept, the teacher must know and be prepared with a plan—to be implemented subsequently—to remedy the situation.

In addition, teachers must be able to analyze their teaching of a lesson in terms of both successes and areas needing improvement. Many lessons—particularly those being taught for the first time—do not proceed exactly as planned. By consciously reflecting on these lessons and analyzing their strong and weak features, teachers are able to learn from their experiences and improve their skills.

In stating what they plan to do subsequently with a group of students, based on what occurred in the observed lesson, teachers provide evidence of their skill in using the results from one lesson to plan for the future. By describing how they might teach the same lesson again, teachers demonstrate their skill in constructively critiquing their own performance. As teachers gain skill in reflection, they can support their judgments with references to specific events in the classroom. If the lesson had more than one goal, the teacher may be able to discuss in comparative terms the degree to which the students as a group achieved the various goals. They may also be able to make and support judgments with respect to the learning of particular individuals or groups of students.

Questions for Assessor Reflection

1. What judgments does the teacher make about the extent to which the goals were met? Are these judgments accurate?

2. How does the teacher support her or his judgment?

3. What explanation does the teacher give for deviations from the instructional plan?

4. How does the teacher analyze the effectiveness of her or his teaching strategies?

5. How does the teacher articulate ways in which insights gained from this lesson could be used to improve future instruction?

D1 Scoring Rules

1.0 The teacher cannot accurately identify strengths and weaknesses of the lesson in relation to the learning goals.

1.5 Above level 1.0, but below level 2.0

2.0 The teacher accurately describes the strengths and weaknesses of the lesson in relation to the learning goals and describes in general terms how he or she could use the experience from this lesson in future instruction.

2.5 Above level 2.0, but below level 3.0

3.0 In addition to the requirements for level 2.0, the teacher supports his or her judgments with specific evidence from the observed lesson.

3.5 Above level 3.0

D2 Demonstrating a sense of efficacy

Description

A teacher who has a sense of efficacy attributes the degree of students' success in meeting learning goals to factors within the classroom rather than to factors outside it. This criterion focuses on the ways in which teachers demonstrate and act on that belief.

Teachers with a high degree of efficacy regard student difficulties in learning as challenges to their own creativity and ingenuity. They actively search for better techniques to help students learn. Thus, a teacher with a high degree of efficacy is not expected to know all the answers to reaching every student, but he or she will persist in looking for alternatives. On the other hand, teachers with little sense of efficacy tend to use factors such as the school administration, excessive television viewing, students' families, or the students themselves as excuses for not persisting in efforts to help students learn.

Teachers with a high sense of efficacy are not expected to have a complete plan to deal with every student's difficulties in learning, particularly immediately after an observed lesson. However, these teachers are prepared with several possible actions, and convey a sense of commitment to persisting in the search for an effective approach so every student can meet the learning goals.

As teachers gain skill in this area, they become more resourceful and their repertoire of possible approaches or actions to try broadens.

Questions for Assessor Reflection

1. In what ways does the teacher convey a sense of efficacy with respect to students' learning?

2. What specific actions does the teacher suggest for working with individual students who are not meeting the learning goals?

D2 Scoring Rules

1.0 The teacher makes no attempt to find ways to help students who are not meeting the learning goals.

1.5 Above level 1.0, but below level 2.0

2.0 The teacher attempts to find ways to help specific students who are not meeting the learning goals, but cannot suggest any specific, practical actions that he or she has not already tried.

2.5 Above level 2.0, but below level 3.0

3.0 The teacher suggests specific, practical actions that he or she intends to take to help specific students who are not meeting the learning goals.

3.5 Above level 3.0

D3 Building professional relationships with colleagues to share teaching insights and to coordinate learning activities for students

Description

This criterion focuses on two distinct, though related, aspects of a teacher's professional relationships with colleagues. The first of these is seeking help from other professionals on matters related to learning and instruction or to other concerns related to teaching. For example, the teacher should know who in the school is experienced in working with students of the same level or in the same subject area, and should be aware of other people in the school or district who can help the teacher improve his or her instructional skills. The teacher should also be aware of others—for example, librarians or specialist teachers—who can provide assistance with curricular materials or other resources to enrich the learning experience for students.

Secondly, the teacher should be aware of how, and with whom, he or she could or should coordinate plans, schedules, and resources for the benefit of the entire class or individual students. As teachers gain skill, they are able to collaborate effectively with colleagues. Examples of such collaboration might include working with other teachers to design integrated lessons or units, coordinating plans with specialists such as ESL teachers, and maintaining close contact with special education teachers for mainstreamed students, and so on. Teachers who team-teach should demonstrate knowledge of how to coordinate activities with colleagues other than the team-teaching partner.

Questions for Assessor Reflection

1. Does the teacher identify colleagues within the school who can provide instructional help that is relevant to the observed lesson or to students in the class?

2. If appropriate, does the teacher identify colleagues whose participation is either necessary or helpful in coordinating learning activities for students?

3. Does the teacher consult with colleagues on matters related to learning and instruction or other professional matters?

4. In what ways does the teacher collaborate with colleagues outside his or her classroom to coordinate learning activities or address other teaching concerns?

D3 Scoring Rules

1.0 The teacher demonstrates no knowledge of resources available through colleagues in the school or district

OR

the teacher is aware of such resources, but does not attempt to use them, despite an obvious need.

1.5 Above level 1.0, but below level 2.0

2.0 The teacher demonstrates knowledge of resources and attempts to consult with colleagues when necessary on matters related to learning and instruction.

2.5 Above level 2.0, but below level 3.0

3.0 In addition to the requirements for level 2.0, the teacher collaborates with colleagues outside of his or her own classroom to coordinate learning activities or to address other concerns related to teaching.

3.5 Above level 3.0

D4 Communicating with parents or guardians about student learning

Description

This criterion focuses on the teacher's contacts with the parents or guardians of students. The nature of communications with parents or guardians regarding the school success of their children will vary significantly with age or grade level and the subject being taught. Potential forms of communication might include, for example, scheduled conferences with parents, telephone calls or written notes about positive events as well as individual students' problems, or class newsletters. For teachers who have instructional contact with large numbers of students, the realistic possibilities will be somewhat more limited than for teachers in self-contained classrooms. Even undifferentiated means of communication—for example, notification of special events such as plays, exhibitions, sports events—can constitute communication with students' parents or guardians.

In all cases, such communication should be handled in a nonthreatening way that is respectful of the cultural diversity in the community. For example, teachers should be sensitive to the effects that a call to a parent at work could have, and should be aware of whether communication exclusively in English is reasonable.

As teachers gain skill, their familiarity with forms of communication should broaden, and they should become more knowledge about which forms are likely to be effective in a particular situation.

Questions for Assessor Reflection

1. Does the teacher demonstrate knowledge of how he or she could communicate with parents or guardians?

2. Does the teacher communicate appropriately with parents or guardians in ways that are suitable for his or her teaching situation?

D4 Scoring Rules

1.0 The teacher demonstrates no knowledge of forms of communication that she or he can use to communicate with parents or guardians

OR

the teacher makes no attempt to communicate with parents or guardians, even when it is clearly necessary to do so.

1.5 Above level 1.0, but below level 2.0

2.0 The teacher demonstrates knowledge of forms of communication that she or he can use to communicate with parents or guardians of students for various purposes.

2.5 Above level 2.0, below level 3.0

3.0 In addition to the requirements for level 2.0, the teacher describes situations in which she or he has communicated or would communicate with parents or guardians regarding specific students and indicates the forms of communication she or he has used or would use.

3.5 Above level 3.0

Appendix B

ASSESSOR PROFILE

Assessor ID #: _____   Social Security #: _____ - _____ - _____

Last Name: _____   First Name: _____ MI: _____

School/Organization: _____   District: _____

Work Address: _____

City: _____ State: _____ Zip: _____ Telephone #: (____)_____

Home Address: _____

City: _____ State: _____ Zip: _____ Telephone #: (____)_____

Please use a **PEN** and **CHECK (✔)** or **PRINT** your responses in the space provided. Unless otherwise indicated, check only one response for each question. Please respond to all questions.

1. What is your age?
   - ○ a. Under 25
   - ○ b. 25 - 34
   - ○ c. 35 - 44
   - ○ d. 45 - 54
   - ○ e. 55 - 64
   - ○ f. 64 or over

2. What is your gender?
   - ○ a. Female
   - ○ b. Male

3. How do you describe yourself?
   - ○ a. African American or Black
   - ○ b. Asian American/Asian (Ex.: Japanese, Chinese, Korean)
   - ○ c. Southeast Asian American/Southeast Asian (Ex.: Cambodian, Hmong, Khmer, Laotian, Vietnamese)
   - ○ d. Pacific Island American/Pacific Islander
   - ○ e. Mexican, Mexican American, or Chicano
   - ○ f. Puerto Rican
   - ○ g. Other Hispanic, Latino, or Latin American
   - ○ h. Native American, American Indian, or Alaskan Native
   - ○ i. White
   - ○ j. Other (please specify) _____

Question 4 - 7

Please provide the following information regarding your **ACADEMIC BACKGROUND**. (Check and complete **ALL** that apply.)

4. Bachelor's degree
   - ○ a. Not begun
   - ○ b. In progress
   - ○ c. Completed

   Major (please specify) _____

   Minor (please specify) _____

5. Master's degree or equivalent
   - ○ a. Not begun
   - ○ b. In progress
   - ○ c. Completed

   Major (please specify) _____

6. Doctorate or equivalent
   - ○ a. Not begun
   - ○ b. In progress
   - ○ c. Completed

   Major (please specify) _____

7. Did you go through an alternate-route teacher training program?
   - ○ a. Yes
   - ○ b. No

155

8. Which of the following best describes your **CURRENT STATUS?**

- ○ a. Emergency/temporary teacher license
- ○ b. Regular teacher, classroom (licensed, not a substitute)
- ○ c. Regular teacher, special assignment
- ○ d. Substitute teacher
- ○ e. Principal or assistant principal
- ○ f. School administrator, other than principal or assistant
- ○ g. Supervisor
- ○ h. State administrator
- ○ i. College faculty
- ○ j. Retired
- ○ k. Other (please specify) _____

9. How many **YEARS** have you taught, including the current year?

- ○ a. Less than 1 year
- ○ b. 1 - 2 years
- ○ c. 3 - 4 years
- ○ d. 5 - 6 years
- ○ e. 7 - 8 years
- ○ f. 9 - 10 years
- ○ g. 10 or more years

10. Which of the following best describes the type of **SCHOOL** in which you are teaching **OR** have taught for the most part of your teaching career, if you are not currently teaching?

- ○ a. Primary elementary
- ○ b. Upper elementary
- ○ c. Comprehensive elementary
- ○ d. Middle
- ○ e. Junior high
- ○ f. Senior high
- ○ g. Comprehensive secondary
- ○ h. Post-secondary
- ○ i. Other (please specify) _____

11. Which of the following best describes the **LEVEL** that you are teaching **OR** have taught for the most part of your teaching career, if you are not currently teaching?

- ○ a. Pre-Kindergarten - Grade 2
- ○ b. Grades 3 - 5
- ○ c. Grades 6 - 8
- ○ d. Grades 9 - 12
- ○ e. More than one of the levels above (please specify)_____

12. Which of the following best describes the **CONTENT** that you are teaching **OR** have taught for the most part of your teaching career, if you are not currently teaching?

- ○ a. All or most elementary school subjects
- ○ b. All or most middle school subjects
- ○ c. Business
- ○ d. Computer science
- ○ e. English as a second language
- ○ f. Foreign language
- ○ g. Health/physical education
- ○ h. Home economics
- ○ i. Language arts/communications
- ○ j. Mathematics
- ○ k. Physical/biological/chemical sciences
- ○ l. Social sciences
- ○ m. Special education
- ○ n. Visual arts/music/theatre/dance
- ○ o. Vocational education
- ○ p. Other (please specify)_____

13. In which fields and levels are you currently **LICENSED** in this state? (Indicate **ALL** categories that apply by using the codes listed on the next page.)

SUBJECT	LEVEL
a. _____	_____
b. _____	_____
c. _____	_____
d. _____	_____
e. _____	_____
f. _____	_____
g. _____	_____
h. _____	_____
i. _____	_____
j. _____	_____

14. Which of the following describes your experience in **EVALUATING** teachers' performance? (Indicate the number of years of experience for each situation that applies.)

- ___ a. No experience
- ___ b. Supervisor of classroom teachers
- ___ c. Supervisor of student teachers
- ___ d. Cooperating teacher
- ___ e. Mentor
- ___ f. School administrator
- ___ g. Other (please specify)_____

LICENSING FIELDS AND LEVELS

EDUCATION SUBJECT AREAS
101 Agricultural Education
102 Art Education
103 Bilingual and Bicultural Education
104 Business Education
105 Cooperative Education
106 English Education
107 Environmental Education
108 Health Education
109 Home Economics Educations
110 Industrial Arts
111 Life Science Education
112 Marketing and Distributive Education
113 Mathematics Education
114 Music Education
115 Office Technology Education
116 Physical Education
117 Physical Science Education
118 Reading Education
119 Reading Specialist
120 Secretarial Education
121 Social Studies Education
122 Teaching English as a Foreign Language
199 Other (please specify)

ELEMENTARY AND PRE-ELEMENTARY EDUCATION
201 Early Childhood Education
202 Elementary Education
203 Pre-Elementary Education
299 Other (please specify)

HUMANITIES
301 Art
302 Drama
303 English
304 Fine Arts
305 French
306 German
307 Italian
308 Japanese
309 Latin
310 Literature
311 Music
312 Philosophy, Religion, or Theology
313 Russian
314 Spanish
315 Speech Communication
316 Writing
399 Other (please specify)

MATHEMATICS AND NATURAL SCIENCES
401 Biology
402 Botany
403 Chemistry
404 Computer and Information Sciences
405 Earth/Space Science
406 Engineering
407 Engineering Technologies
408 General Science
409 Geology
410 Mathematics
411 Physics
499 Other (please specify)

NON-TEACHING EDUCATION
501 Educational Administration
502 Educational Psychology
503 Library and Archival Sciences
504 School Guidance/Counseling
505 School Psychology
506 School Social Work
507 Supervision
599 Other (please specify)

SOCIAL SCIENCES
601 Anthropology
602 Business
603 Communications
604 Economics
605 Geography
606 Government
607 History
608 Political Science
609 Psychology
610 Public Affairs and Services
611 Social Studies
612 Sociology
699 Other (please specify)

SPECIAL EDUCATION
701 Audiology
702 Education of Students with Mental Retardation
703 Reading Education
704 Special Education
705 Speech Language Pathology
706 Teaching Speech to Students with Language Disabilities
707 Teaching Students with Emotional Disabilities
708 Teaching Students with Hearing Disabilities
709 Teaching Students with Learning Disabilities
710 Teaching Students with Minimal Mental Disabilities
711 Teaching Students with Orthopedic Disabilities
712 Teaching Students with Physical and Mental Disabilities
713 Teaching Students with Visual Disabilities
799 Other (please specify)

VOCATIONAL/TECHNICAL MAJORS
801 Accounting
802 Agriculture
803 Architecture and Environmental Design
804 Home Economics
805 Military Sciences
806 Office Technology
899 Other (please specify)

LEVELS
001 K - 6
002 K - 8
003 7 - 12
004 9 - 12
005 K - 12
006 Other (please specify)

CANDIDATE PROFILE

Candidate ID #: _____   Social Security #: _____ - _____ - _____

Last Name: _____   First Name: _____ MI: _____

School/Organization: _____   District: _____

Work Address: _____

City: _____ State: _____ Zip: _____ Telephone #: (____)_____

Home Address: _____

City: _____ State: _____ Zip: _____ Telephone #: (____)_____

Please use a **PEN** and **CHECK** (✔) or **PRINT** your responses in the space provided. Unless otherwise indicated, check only one response for each question. Please respond to all questions.

1. What is your age?
   - ○ a. Under 25
   - ○ b. 25 - 34
   - ○ c. 35 - 44
   - ○ d. 45 - 54
   - ○ e. 55 - 64
   - ○ f. 65 or over

2. What is your gender?
   - ○ a. Female
   - ○ b. Male

3. How do you describe yourself?
   - ○ a. African American or Black
   - ○ b. Asian American/Asian (Ex.: Japanese, Chinese, Korean)
   - ○ c. Southeast Asian American/Southeast Asian (Ex.: Cambodian, Hmong, Khmer, Laotian, Vietnamese)
   - ○ d. Pacific Island American/Pacific Islander
   - ○ e. Mexican, Mexican American, or Chicano
   - ○ f. Puerto Rican
   - ○ g. Other Hispanic, Latino, or Latin American
   - ○ h. Native American, American Indian, or Alaskan Native
   - ○ i. White
   - ○ j. Other (please specify) _____

Question 4 - 7

Please provide the following information regarding your **ACADEMIC BACKGROUND**. (Check and complete **ALL** that apply.)

4. Bachelor's degree
   - ○ a. Not begun
   - ○ b. In progress
   - ○ c. Completed

   Major (please specify) _____
   Minor (please specify) _____

5. Master's degree or equivalent
   - ○ a. Not begun
   - ○ b. In progress
   - ○ c. Completed

   Major (please specify) _____

6. Doctorate or equivalent
   - ○ a. Not begun
   - ○ b. In progress
   - ○ c. Completed

   Major (please specify) _____

7. Are you going through an alternate-route teacher training program?
   - ○ a. Yes
   - ○ b. No

8. Which of the following best describes the type of **SCHOOL** in which you are **CURRENTLY** teaching?

   O   a. Primary elementary
   O   b. Upper elementary
   O   c. Comprehensive elementary
   O   d. Middle
   O   e. Junior high
   O   f. Senior high
   O   g. Comprehensive secondary
   O   h. Other (please specify) _____

9. Which of the following best describes the **LEVEL** of your primary teaching assignment?

   O   a. Pre-Kindergarten - Grade 2
   O   b. Grades 3-5
   O   c. Grades 6-8
   O   d. Grades 9-12
   O   e. More than one of the levels above (please specify) _____

10. Which of the following best describes the **CONTENT** of your primary teaching assignment?

    O   a. All or most elementary school subjects
    O   b. All or most middle school subjects
    O   c. Business
    O   d. Computer science
    O   e. English as a second language
    O   f. Foreign language
    O   g. Health/physical education
    O   h. Home economics
    O   i. Language arts/communications
    O   j. Mathematics
    O   k. Physical/biological/chemical sciences
    O   l. Social sciences
    O   m. Special education
    O   n. Visual arts/music/theatre/dance
    O   o. Vocational education
    O   p. Other (please specify) _____

11. Which of the following best describes your **CURRENT STATUS?**

    O   a. Temporary substitute teacher (assigned on a daily basis)
    O   b. Permanent substitute teacher (assigned on a long- term basis)
    O   c. Teacher with emergency/temporary license
    O   d. Student teacher
    O   e. First-year teacher
    O   f. Teacher with one or more years of experience
    O   g. Other (please specify) _____

12. From what institution have you received or will you be receiving your education **DEGREE?** (Indicate the name of the school that applies and use the codes listed on the next page)

    _____   _____

    Name of school   Code

160

School Codes

001   Delaware State University

002   University of Delaware

003   Wesley College

004   Wilmington College

[This list will be tailored for each state.]

CLASS PROFILE

Candidate Name:_____ Candidate ID # _____ Social Security # ___-___-___

School _____ District:_____

Grade(s)_____ Subject(s) _____ Room #/Location _____ Date of Observation ____/____/____
                                                                                        Month Date Year

Number of Assessors Present for Observation _____

Please use a **PEN** and **CHECK** (✔) or **PRINT** your responses in the space provided. Unless otherwise indicated, check only one response for each question. Please respond to all questions.

---

1. Which of the following best describes the **LEVEL** of the class being observed?
   - O a. Pre-Kindergarten - Grade 2
   - O b. Grades 3-5
   - O c. Grades 6-8
   - O d. Grades 9-12
   - O e. More than one of the levels above
     (please specify)_____

2. Which of the following best describes the **CONTENT** of the class being observed?
   - O a. Business
   - O b. Computer science
   - O c. English as a second language
   - O d. Foreign language
   - O e. Health/physical education
   - O f. Home economics
   - O g. Language arts/communications
   - O h. Mathematics
   - O i. Physical/biological/chemical sciences
   - O j. Social sciences
   - O k. Special education
   - O l. Visual arts/music/theater/dance
   - O m. Vocational education
   - O n. Other (please specify) _____

3. Which of the following best describes the areas from which your students come? (Check **ALL** that apply.)
   - O a. Low income, urban
   - O b. Middle or upper income, urban
   - O c. Low income, suburban
   - O d. Middle or upper income, suburban
   - O e. Low income, small town (not suburban)
   - O f. Middle or upper income, small town (not suburban)
   - O g. Low income, rural
   - O h. Middle or upper income, rural

4. [   ] What is the **TOTAL NUMBER** of students enrolled in the class to be observed?

5. [   ] a. What is the number of **MALE** students?

   [   ] b. What is the number of **FEMALE** students?

6. [   ] What is the **AGE** range for all of the students in the class?

7. What is the estimated number of students identified in each **RACIAL/ETHNIC GROUP**?
   - [   ] a. African American or Black
   - [   ] b. Asian American/Asian
     [Ex.: Japanese, Chinese, Korean)
   - [   ] c. Southeast Asian American/ Southeast Asian
     (Ex.: Cambodian, Hmong, Khmer, Laotian, Vietnamese)
   - [   ] d. Pacific Island American/Pacific Islander
   - [   ] e. Mexican, Mexican American, or Chicano
   - [   ] f. Puerto Rican
   - [   ] g. Other Hispanic, Latino, or Latin American
   - [   ] h. Native American, American Indian, or Alaskan Native
   - [   ] i. White
   - [   ] j. Other (please specify)

8. What is the estimated number of students in each of the following **LANGUAGE** categories?
   - [   ] a. English language proficient
   - [   ] b. Limited English language proficient

9. Approximately what **PERCENTAGE** of your class can be categorized as the following?

(Percentage)

[   ] a. Above-average or advanced skill level

[   ] b. Average or intermediate skill level

[   ] c. Below-average skill level

100%   Total

10. Approximately how many students in this class have been identified as having **EXCEPTIONALITIES**?

[   ] a. Blind or visually impaired

[   ] b. Deaf or hearing impaired

[   ] c. Developmentally disabled

[   ] d. Emotionally or behaviorally disabled

[   ] e. Gifted

[   ] f. Learning disabled

[   ] g. Physically disabled

[   ] h. Other (please specify) _____

11. Is there anything about the **LEARNING ENVIRONMENT** that you think might affect your students or the scheduled observation (e.g., this is not your own classroom; there is a new display, pet, or equipment in the room; there is construction going on in the building)? If so, please note.

12. What are the most important CLASSROOM ROUTINES, PROCEDURES, RULES and EXPECTATIONS FOR STUDENT BEHAVIOR that will be in operation during the observed lesson (e.g., collecting papers, reviewing homework, safety precautions)?

13. Are there any **CIRCUMSTANCES** that the assessor should be aware of in order to understand what will occur during the scheduled observation (e.g., use of schoolwide discipline, schoolwide policies, interruptions, behavior patterns of certain students)? If so, please explain.

14. In the space below, please provide a simple **SKETCH** of the arrangement of the instructional space for this lesson (e.g., student desks, teacher desk, student work space, arrangement of playing field or laboratory). Please attach a **SEATING CHART** with the students' names, if available, or a **LIST** of students for the class to be observed.

INSTRUCTION PROFILE

Candidate Name:_____ Candidate ID # _____ Social Security # ____-__-____

Subject: _____ Grade:_____

Date of Observation ____/____/____

Month　Date　Year

Please use a **PEN** and **PRINT** your responses in the space provided. Respond to all questions.

1. What are your **GOALS** for student learning for this class period? In other words, what changes do you hope will occur in the students as a result of this class period? Include learning goals in any domain that is relevant to the lesson (e.g., academic, social, affective, cognitive, aesthetic, and/or psychomotor goals).

2. Where appropriate in **PLANNING THIS LESSON**, how have you used or accommodated the diverse experiences, related to the categories listed below, that your students bring to class?

    a. Gender

    b. Race/ethnicity

    c. English language proficiency

    d. Economic status

    e. Skill level

    f. Exceptionalities

3. How does the **CONTENT** of this lesson build on what has been learned **PREVIOUSLY**?

4. How does the **CONTENT** of this lesson relate to what students will be learning in the **FUTURE**?

5. What teaching **METHODS** have you selected to help you achieve your learning goals (e.g., teacher presentation, peer teaching, programmed instruction, etc.)?

6. What learning **ACTIVITIES** have you planned for this class (e.g., game to learn map skills, drawing the action in a story, quiz, etc.)? Briefly outline the sequence of activities and indicate approximately how much time you plan to spend on each.

Activity   *Allocated Time*

7. What instructional **MATERIALS**, if any, will you use to help your students reach the specified learning goals? *If appropriate*, please **STAPLE** to this form a copy of any student **MATERIALS** you plan to use with this class (e.g., map, vocabulary list, questions to be answered, printed instructions, homework).

8. If you will be **GROUPING** students for this class period, please provide the following information.

   a. Group Name or Number   Number of Students   Basis for Group Membership

   b. Is this a **TYPICAL** grouping pattern for this class? If not, please explain.

9. How will you know that the students have learned what you intended them to learn? *If appropriate*, please **STAPLE** to this form a copy of your **EVALUATION PLAN** or **INSTRUMENT** (e.g., a list of oral questions, written quiz, student demonstration of a skill, or any other evaluation strategy you plan to use).

Candidate Name:_____ Candidate ID # _____ Social Security #_____-___-_____

Assessor Name: _____ Assessor ID # _____ Social Security #_____-___-_____

Date of Observation____/____/_____ Start Time of Interview____/____ End Time of Interview____/____
            Month Date Year   Hour Minute   Hour Minute

(Introduce yourself and explain the purpose of the interview.)

1. I've reviewed your **CLASS** and **INSTRUCTION** Profiles. Please take a few moments to look them over and tell me if there have been any changes in these since you completed them.

---

*(Review the candidate's **GOALS** from the **INSTRUCTION PROFILE** (question 1) with the candidate and probe for clarity, making notations directly on the **INSTRUCTION PROFILE** form. Then ask the candidate the following question.)*

2. Why have you chosen these **GOALS?**

---

3. How do the connections between this lesson past learning and future learning reflect the **ORGANIZATION** of the **SUBJECT** or **DISCIPLINE** as a whole?

169

4a. What **PRIOR KNOWLEDGE** and **SKILLS** do students need in order to be successful in reaching the goal(s) of the lesson?

b. How do you become **FAMILIAR** with the **PRIOR KNOWLEDGE** and **SKILLS** your students bring to this and other lessons?

(Review Question 2 in the INSTRUCTION PROFILE with the candidate and ask the following question.)

5a. How do you become **FAMILIAR** with your students' **CULTURAL RESOURCES** (e.g., experiences outside of school, approaches to learning, styles of interacting and relating)?

b. How does this lesson accommodate and use your students' **CULTURAL RESOURCES**?

c. Why are the accommodations you have made **IMPORTANT** to student learning?

(Review the TEACHING METHODS from the INSTRUCTION PROFILE (question 5) with the candidate and probe for clarity, making notations directly on the INSTRUCTION PROFILE form. Then ask the candidate the following question.)

6. Why have you chosen these **TEACHING METHODS**?
   (**EXPLORE** the relationship to the stated **LEARNING GOALS** and to the background and experiences of the **STUDENTS** in the class.)

*(Review the learning **ACTIVITIES** from the **INSTRUCTION PROFILE** (question 6) with the candidate and probe for clarity, making notations directly on the **INSTRUCTION PROFILE** form. Then ask the candidate the following question.)*

7. Why have you chosen these particular learning **ACTIVITIES**? (**EXPLORE** the relationship to the stated **LEARNING GOALS** and to the background and experiences of the **STUDENTS** in the class.)

*(Review **MATERIALS** the candidate has identified in the **INSTRUCTION PROFILE** (question 7) and probe for clarity, making notations directly on the **INSTRUCTION PROFILE** form. Then ask the candidate the following question.)*

8. Why have you chosen these **INSTRUCTIONAL MATERIALS**? (**EXPLORE** the relationship to the stated **LEARNING GOALS** and to the background and experiences of the **STUDENTS** in the class.)

*(Review the **EVALUATION PLAN** from the **INSTRUCTION PROFILE** (question 9) and probe for clarity, making notations directly on the **INSTRUCTION PROFILE** form. Then ask the candidate the following questions.)*

9a. Why have you chosen to **EVALUATE** student learning using the strategies you've described? (**EXPLORE** the relationship to the stated **LEARNING GOALS** and to the **STUDENTS** in the class.)

9b. If student outcomes are not going to be evaluated today, when will this occur? (Ask the candidate to describe **FUTURE** evaluation.)

CLASS OBSERVATION RECORD

Page ___1___ of ____ pages

Candidate Name:_____   Candidate ID #_____ Date of Obs. ____/____/____
                                                                          Month   Date   Year
Assessor Name: _____   Assessor ID # _____

Time	Comments		Code
		(1)	
		(2)	
		(3)	
		(4)	
		(5)	
		(6)	
		(7)	
		(8)	
		(9)	
		(10)	
		(11)	
		(12)	
		(13)	
		(14)	
		(15)	
		(16)	
		(17)	
		(18)	
		(19)	
		(20)	
		(21)	
		(22)	
		(23)	
		(24)	
		(25)	
		(26)	

CLASS OBSERVATION RECORD (CONT'D.)

Candidate Name:_____   Candidate ID #_____ Date of Obs. ____/____/_____

Assessor Name: _____   Assessor ID # _____

                                                  Month   Date   Year

Time	Comments		Code
		(1)	
		(2)	
		(3)	
		(4)	
		(5)	
		(6)	
		(7)	
		(8)	
		(9)	
		(10)	
		(11)	
		(12)	
		(13)	
		(14)	
		(15)	
		(16)	
		(17)	
		(18)	
		(19)	
		(20)	
		(21)	
		(22)	
		(23)	
		(24)	
		(25)	
		(26)	
		(27)	
		(28)	

POSTOBSERVATION INTERVIEW

Candidate Name:_____ Candidate ID # _____ Social Security #_____-___-_____

Assessor Name: _____ Assessor ID # _____ Social Security #_____-___-_____

Date of Observation____/____/____ Start Time of Interview____/____ End Time of Interview____/____
             Month Date Year   Hour Minute   Hour Minute

---

*1a. (Review the information on **INSTRUCTIONAL GOALS** from the **INSTRUCTION PROFILE** and the **PREOBSERVATION INTERVIEW**.)*

In light of your **INSTRUCTIONAL GOALS**, how do you think the lesson went?

b. Did the students learn what you wanted them to learn? How do you know that the students learned or did not learn what you wanted them to learn?

*(Make certain that the candidate **COMMENTS** on each **LEARNING GOAL** noted in the Instruction Profile.)*

c. Were the teaching **METHODS** effective? How do you know they were or were not effective?

d. Were the **ACTIVITIES** you used helpful? How do you know they were or were not helpful?

e. Were the **MATERIALS** you used helpful? How do you know they were or were not helpful?

---

2. Did you **DEPART** from anything you had planned to do during this class period? If so, when and why?

3. If you could teach this class period over again to the same class:

a. What would you do **DIFFERENTLY**? Why?
   (Probe for specific evidence.)

b. What would you do the **SAME**? Why?
   (Probe for specific evidence.)

4. Based on what happened today, what do you plan to do **NEXT** with this class?
   (Probe for specific ideas or plans.)

(Note an INDIVIDUAL or GROUP of students who appeared to be DOING WELL with the instructional tasks; then ask the candidate the following questions.)

5a. How do you think _____ performed today?

b. How do you account for this performance?

c. What might you try in the future with _____ ?

(Note an INDIVIDUAL or GROUP of students who appeared to be HAVING PROBLEMS with the instructional tasks; then ask the candidate the following questions.)

6a. How do you think _____ performed today?

b   How do you account for this performance?

c. What might you try in the future with _____ ?

7. When you need **ASSISTANCE** with your teaching skills, or when you have **PROBLEMS** with a particular student, whom do you talk with?

8. Do you **COORDINATE** learning activities with other teachers? If so, why and how?

9a. What forms of **COMMUNICATION** do you use with the **PARENTS OR GUARDIANS** of the students in this class?

b. How and under what conditions do you use them?

10. Is there **ANYTHING ELSE** you feel I should know about today's lesson?

11. I have several questions about the lesson.
(This is your last opportunity to ask questions about any information collected during the assessment cycle for which you need clarification.)

RECORD OF EVIDENCE

Candidate Name:_____ Candidate ID # _____ Social Security # ____-___-____

Assessor Name: _____ Assessor ID #_____ Disctrict: _____

School:_____ District: _____

Grade(s)_____ Subject(s) _____

Date of Observation____/____/_____ Start Time of Observation____/_____ End Time of Observation____/_____
　　　　　　　　　Month　Date　Year　　　　　　　　　　　　　　Hour　Minute　　　　　　　　　　　　　Hour　Minute

Number of Assessors Present for Observation _____

A. ORGANIZING CONTENT KNOWLEDGE FOR STUDENT LEARNING

Evaluation

A1. Becoming familiar with relevant aspects of students' background,   1.0   1.5   2.0   2.5   3.0   3.5
knowledge and experiences   ☐   ☐   ☐   ☐   ☐   ☐

Summary Statement:

A2. Articulating clear learning goals for the lesson that are appropriate   1.0   1.5   2.0   2.5   3.0   3.5
for the students   ☐   ☐   ☐   ☐   ☐   ☐

Summary Statement:

179

A. ORGANIZING CONTENT KNOWLEDGE FOR STUDENT LEARNING (cont'd)

A3. Demonstrating an understanding of the connections between the content that was learned previously, the current content, and the content that remains to be learned in the future

1.0	1.5	2.0	2.5	3.0	3.5
☐	☐	☐	☐	☐	☐

Summary Statement:

A4. Creating or selecting teaching methods, learning activities and instructional materials or other resources that are appropriate for the students and that are aligned with the goals of the lesson

1.0	1.5	2.0	2.5	3.0	3.5
☐	☐	☐	☐	☐	☐

Teaching methods:

Learning activities:

Instructional materials and resources:

Summary Statement:

180

A. ORGANIZING CONTENT KNOWLEDGE FOR STUDENT LEARNING (cont'd)

	1.0	1.5	2.0	2.5	3.0	3.5
A5. Creating or selecting evaluation strategies that are appropriate for the students and that are aligned with the goals of the lesson	☐	☐	☐	☐	☐	☐

Summary Statement:

Use this space for any additional comments on the criteria in Domain A.

B. CREATING AN ENVIRONMENT FOR STUDENT LEARNING

	1.0	1.5	2.0	2.5	3.0	3.5
B1. Creating a climate that promotes fairness	☐	☐	☐	☐	☐	☐

Summary Statement:

	1.0	1.5	2.0	2.5	3.0	3.5
B2. Establishing and maintaining rapport with students	☐	☐	☐	☐	☐	☐

Summary Statement:

B. CREATING AN ENVIRONMENT FOR STUDENT LEARNING (cont'd)

B3. Communicating challenging learning expectations to each student

1.0	1.5	2.0	2.5	3.0	3.5
☐	☐	☐	☐	☐	☐

Summary Statement:

B4. Establishing and maintaining consistent standards of classroom behavior

1.0	1.5	2.0	2.5	3.0	3.5
☐	☐	☐	☐	☐	☐

Summary Statement:

183

B. CREATING AN ENVIRONMENT FOR STUDENT LEARNING (cont'd)

	1.0	1.5	2.0	2.5	3.0	3.5
B5. Making the physical environment as safe and conducive to learning as possible	☐	☐	☐	☐	☐	☐

Summary Statement:

Use this space for any additional comments on the criteria in Domain B.

184

C. TEACHING FOR STUDENT LEARNING

C1. Making learning goals and instructional procedures clear to students	1.0	1.5	2.0	2.5	3.0	3.5
	☐	☐	☐	☐	☐	☐

Summary Statement:

C2. Making content comprehensible to students	1.0	1.5	2.0	2.5	3.0	3.5
	☐	☐	☐	☐	☐	☐

Summary Statement:

185

C. TEACHING FOR STUDENT LEARNING (cont'd)

C3. Encouraging students to extend their thinking

1.0	1.5	2.0	2.5	3.0	3.5
☐	☐	☐	☐	☐	☐

Summary Statement:

C4. Monitoring students' understanding of content through a variety of means, providing feedback to students to assist learning, and adjusting learning activities as the situation demands

1.0	1.5	2.0	2.5	3.0	3.5
☐	☐	☐	☐	☐	☐

Monitoring understanding:

Providing feedback:

Adjusting learning activities:

Summary Statement:

186

C. TEACHING FOR STUDENT LEARNING (cont'd)

	1.0	1.5	2.0	2.5	3.0	3.5
C5. Using instructional time effectively	☐	☐	☐	☐	☐	☐

Summary Statement:

Use this space for any additional comments on the criteria in Domain C.

D. TEACHER PROFESSIONALISM

D1. Reflecting on the extent to which the learning goals were met	1.0	1.5	2.0	2.5	3.0	3.5
	☐	☐	☐	☐	☐	☐

Summary Statement:

D2. Demonstrating a sense of efficacy	1.0	1.5	2.0	2.5	3.0	3.5
	☐	☐	☐	☐	☐	☐

Summary Statement:

188

D. TEACHER PROFESSIONALISM (cont'd)

D3. Building professional relationships with colleagues to share
teaching insights and coordinate learning activities for students

1.0	1.5	2.0	2.5	3.0	3.5
☐	☐	☐	☐	☐	☐

Summary Statement:

D4. Communicating with parents or guardians about student learning

1.0	1.5	2.0	2.5	3.0	3.5
☐	☐	☐	☐	☐	☐

Summary Statement:

189

Use this space for any additional comments on the criteria in Domain D.

Appendix C

PRAXIS III
Outline of Assessor Training

	DAY ONE	DAY TWO	DAY THREE	DAY FOUR	DAY FIVE
MORNING	Introduction • overview • the assessment process Examining Assumptions • approaches to teaching • instructional activity • models of organization and instruction • assumption about learning and teaching	Interviewing Skills • skill development • practice Documenting Domain A • preobservation conference • coding notes • summarizing evidence • making judgments	Taking Notes • abbreviations • watching tape • taking notes Documenting Domain B • coding notes for Domain B Domain C • identifying criteria	Domain D • identify criteria • watching post conference Scoring Domain B & D • coding notes • summarize evidence • making judgments	Review of Field Experience • paired sharing Obstacles to Objectivity • halo • leniency • central tendency Making Complex Judgments • the judgment process • weighing evidence
AFTERNOON	The Domains • identifying the domains • graphing the domains • sources of evidence Domain A • identifying criteria • summarizing evidence • making judgments	Culture of the Classroom • research findings • instructional implications Domain B • identifying criteria • summarizing evidence	Documenting Domain C • summarizing evidence • making judgments	Scoring Domain B & D (con't) Field Experience	Complete Assessment Process • reviewing written materials • watching video of class, conferences • coding notes • summarizing evidence • making judgments

Note: A break of 2-3 weeks is scheduled between days four and five to allow participants the opportunity for a field experience. The assessor proficiency test is administered at a later date.

PRAXIS III TRAINING PROGRAM
REVISED OUTLINE
VERSION I

TOPIC	ACTIVITY	MATERIALS NEEDED
DAY ONE		
1. Introduction (60 min)	a. Overview Trainer presents brief overview of outcomes of the training program, and the organization of Training Manual. Participants introduce themselves. (15)	Transparencies • outcomes • summary agenda
	b. Performance assessment exercise: Participants reflect on experience with being assessed. They then generate principles of successful assessment. Trainer introduces concepts of "halo," "leniency," "central tendency." (15)	Transparencies • obstacles to objectivity
	c. The Assessment Process Trainer presents overview of assessment process, introducing the activities and methods needed to collect information (15)	Introductory Video
	d. Participants share expectations and initial perceptions. (15)	
2. Examining Assumptions (145 min)	a. Approaches to Teaching Trainer shows tape of 2 segments using different teaching styles. Participants complete worksheet 2-a indicating aspects of the instruction they believe represent good and poor teaching. Next, groups compare their findings and prepare a composite summary of elements of the teaching on which they agree and those elements on which they disagree. (worksheet 2-b)	Taped segments • Worksheet 2-a • Worksheet 2-b
	Trainer presents tabulation of pre-training survey and points out the need for a training program to develop shared values and help participants make similar judgments. Participants discuss underlying assumptions, and relate them to the readings sent prior to training. (45)	Transparency • values underlying "PRAXIS III"
BREAK (10 min)		

	b. Instructional activity. Trainer conducts an instructional activity with the group. From this exercise, the group derives the conception of learning underlying PRAXIS III: active, constructivist, and building on prior knowledge. (70)	Materials for activity
	c. Models of Organization & Instruction Classrooms look different. Trainer conducts discussion regarding different models of organization. Explains matrix. Participants fill in cells from taped segments in Topic 2-a. (30)	Transparency • models of organization & instruction
LUNCH		
3. The Domains (50 min)	a. Trainer provided *brief* overview of domains (5)	Transparency • the Domains
	b. In small groups, participants compare highlighted words on domain descriptions and answers to worksheet; compare answers against key. (10)	1-page summary description, highlighters
	c. In small groups, participants complete worksheet 3-a, check against "answer key", discuss as needed. (10)	
	d. In small groups, participants create graphic representations of the relationships among the domains. (20)	newsprint, markers
	e. Sources of evidence: trainer *briefly* describes the different sources of evidence used in PRAXIS III. Participants identify primary sources of evidence for each of the domains. (5)	Transparencies • Sources of Evidence • Methods of Matrix
4. Domain A, A1 (30 min)	a. Overview: Trainer briefly reviews the criteria in Domain A (5)	Transparency • Domain A
	b. In small groups, participants share highlighted words in A1 description and scoring rules, locate pertinent questions from class and instruction profiles, preobservation interview. (10)	A1 description, Scoring Rules, highlighters
	c. Trainer models preparation of a scoring matrix for A1; participants add to their copy. (5)	
	d. In small groups, participants look at one sample Records of Evidence; assign ratings; share in larger group; trainer clarifies misunderstandings as needed. (10)	Records of Evidence for A1

BREAK (10 min)		
A2 (50 min)	a. Trainer defines "goal". (5)	Transparency • definition of "goal"
	b. Trainer presents distinction between goals and activities: participants do worksheet 4-a, check against answer key; identify goals of instructional activity. (10)	Transparency • activities or goals Worksheet 4-a • activities or goals
	c. In small groups, participants share highlighted words in descriptions and scoring rules; identify A2 questions from instruction profile and preobservation interview and prepare scoring matrix; share in large groups. Trainer clarifies misconceptions. (10)	Scoring Rules, highlighters
	d. Writing summary statements. Participants study summary statements from A1 Records of Evidence. Identify characteristics. (10)	Transparency • Summary Statements
	e. Participants look at one sample Records of Evidence without summary statements, draft a summary statement and determine rating in small groups; mount on wall and discuss as necessary. (15)	A2 Records of Evidence
A3, A4, A5 (60 min)	a. In small groups, participants share highlighted words in descriptions and scoring rules; identify questions form instruction profile and preobservation interview, prepare scoring matrices. Share, clarify as needed. (30)	Instruction Profile Preobservation Conference Interview
	b. Participants look at one sample Record of Evidence for each criterion; draft summary statements and determine rating in small groups; mount on wall and discuss as necessary. (15)	Records of Evidence
	c. Worksheet 4-b: Domain A. Participants compare answers to worksheet, check against "answer key." Discuss as needed. (10)	Worksheet 4-b: Domain A
	d. Note: If it has not arisen spontaneously, the trainer should conduct a discussion at this point of the generic scoring rules. (10)	Transparency • The Rating Scale
END OF DAY ONE		
HOMEWORK: Review Domain B criteria, "Culturally Responsive Pedagogy."		

Day Two		
5. Interviewing Skills (50 min)	a. Trainer briefly explains elements of interviewing. (10)	Interview tape • Worksheet 5-a
	b. Participants watch the Preobservation Conference interview tape in which the interviewer makes "errors". In small groups, participants complete worksheet 5-a; discuss in large group in light of principles of interviewing. (30)	Transparencies • Interviewing Elements • Establishing Rapport • Standardized Delivery • Probing • Interviewing Do's and Don'ts
	c. Probing role-playing. In small groups, participants prepare inadequate answers and suitable probes for one or two questions on the preobservation interview. Present these in role-play to full group; other participants suggest additional probes. (20)	
6. Documenting Domain A (60 min)	a. Participants review Class and Instruction Profiles, watch taped interview of the preobservation interview. (20)	Videotape: Studio Art
	b. Trainer models coding Instruction Profile and interview notes to criteria in Domain A on overhead projector. (10)	Transparencies • Completed Instruction Profile, page 1 • Preobservation Conference, page 1
BREAK (10 min)		
	c. Participants work in pairs to complete coding of all notes to Domain A criteria (20)	
	d. Trainer models process for completing Record of Evidence for A1: • collect all evidence for A1 on the flip chart • determine most important evidence • write general statements on Record of Evidence • read scoring rules; determine best rating • write summary statement (10)	Transparency • Record of Evidence for Domain A
	e. In pairs, participants complete Record of Evidence for remainder of domain A. (20)	
	f. Distribute "answer key", Record of Evidence, Domain A; pairs compare their answers. (20)	
	g. As needed, discuss generic "Step in completing a Record of Evidence," and "Features of a Successful Record of Evidence." (10)	Transparencies • Steps in completing a Record of Evidence • Features of successful Record of Evidence

LUNCH		
7. Culture of the Classroom (70 min)	a. "Barnga". Participants engage in a simulation game designed to illustrate the issue of cross-cultural mis-communication. (45)	Barnga tournament materials
	b. Culture of the classroom: Trainer presents tabulation of pre-training survey regarding classroom culture. Participants share knowledge of diverse student cultural patterns; trainer supplements from research. (15)	
BREAK (10 MIN)		
8. Domain B (95 min)	a. Provide a brief overview of the criteria in Domain B. (5)	Transparency • Domain B
	b. "Jigsaw" activity, with group divided into five small groups. Each group shares highlighted words in description and scoring rule for one of the criteria in depth, preparing scoring matrix and identifies examples of the criteria from their own professional experience. (15)	Worksheet 8-a; Domain B examples
	c. The jigsaw groups re-form, with individuals from each of the first groups. Each individual presents criterion in Domain B. If appropriate, they should act them out. (30)	
	d. Domain B worksheet: in jigsaw groups, participants compare answers to worksheet 8-b, check against "answer key", discuss as needed. (15)	Worksheet 8-b; Domain B
	e. Participants analyze one Record of Evidence for each of the B criteria, draft summary statements and ratings. Compare with "expert" versions. Mount on wall and discuss as needed. (30)	Domain B Records of Evidence, summary statements and ratings
END OF DAY TWO		
HOMEWORK: Review Domain C. Read pp ___; "Take Notes".		

DAY THREE		
9. Taking Notes (60 min)	a. Provide a brief overview of the criteria in Domain B. (5)	Transparency • Domain B.
	b. "Jigsaw" activity, with group divided into five small groups. Each group shares highlighted words in description and scoring rule for one of the criteria in depth, preparing scoring matrix and identifies examples of the criteria from their own professional experience. (15)	Worksheet 8-a; Domain B examples
	c. The jigsaw groups re-form, with individuals from each of the first groups. Each individual presents criterion in Domain B. If appropriate, they should act them out. (30)	
	d. Domain B worksheet: in jigsaw groups, participants compare answers to worksheet 8-b, check against "answer key", discuss as needed. (15)	Worksheet 8-b; Domain B
	e. Participants analyze one Record of Evidence for each of the B criteria, draft summary statements and ratings. Compare with "expert" versions. Mount on wall and discuss as needed. (30)	Domain B Records of Evidence, summary statements and ratings
10. Finding evidence for Domain B (40 min)	a. Trainer models coding "expert" notes to Domain B criteria. Participants complete individually; compare in pairs and with "expert" codes. (30)	Transparency • first page to model coding
	b. Participants make notes of anything they want to ask about in the postobservation interview. (10)	"expert" coding of notes
BREAK		

11. Domain C (145 min)	a. Deficit v. diverse; Trainer explains distinction. Complete transparency with groups eliciting "correct" answers. Discuss as needed. (10)	Transparency • deficit v. difference
	b. Trainer solicits suggestions from group on how to alter instructional and evaluation strategies, on flip chart. Relate the concepts of culturally responsive pedagogy to each of the criteria in Domain A and B. (20)	5 elements from Ana Maria's paper
	c. Trainer *briefly* introduces the criteria in Domain C. (5)	Transparency • Domain C
	d. Small groups are assigned to individual criteria except C4; compare highlighted words in the descriptions and scoring rules, prepare scoring matrices, and identify examples of Domain C criteria from the instructional activity. When groups are investigating individual criteria, they should be alert to possible overlap and confusion with criteria in domains A & B. (20)	Worksheet 11a Handouts for each group describing examples of the C criteria in the activity
	e. Groups presents domain C criteria to the full group. (20)	
LUNCH		
	f. Criterion C4. Teaching for Thinking. Participants identify instructional strategies suitable for teaching for thinking. (30)	
	g. Participants compare answers to Domain C worksheet; discuss individual items as needed. (10)	Worksheet 11b; Domain C
	h. In groups, participants analyze one Record of Evidence for each of the Domain C criteria; write summary statements; determine ratings; mount on wall and discuss as needed. (30)	Prepared Records of Evidence
12. Documenting Domain C (130 min)	a. Trainer shows H. S. English tape; participants take notes. (30)	H. S. English Tape
BREAK		

	b. In groups, participants code notes. (20)	Transparency
	c. Trainer models completing the Record of Evidence for criterion C1. (10)	• Record of Evidence, C1
	d. Participants complete Record of Evidence for other C criteria individually, compare in pairs and with completed record. Trainer clarifies as needed. (60)	Completed Record of Evidence for all B criteria
	e. Review, as needed, "Features of a Successful Record of Evidence". (10)	Transparency
END DAY THREE		

DAY FOUR		
13. Domain D (95 min)	a. Trainer *briefly* introduces the criteria in Domain D (5)	Transparency • Domain D
	b. Participants share highlighted words in descriptions and scoring rules of criteria; prepare scoring matrices, compare answers on worksheet 13-a. Trainer conducts discussion and clarifies misconceptions, as needed. (45)	
	c. In small group, participants analyze one Record of Evidence for each criterion in Domain D; write summary statements; determine ratings; compare with "expert" (20)	Prepared Records of Evidence for Domain D criteria
BREAK (10 min)		
	d. Post-conference. Participants review their notes from the Studio Art Class and questions that they hope are answered in the Postobservation Conference. (10)	
	e. Participants watch the post conference tape. (15)	Studio Art tape
12. Documenting Domain B and D (95 min)	a. Record of Evidence, Domain B: Trainer models completing the Record of Evidence for B1, listing important evidence on the flip chart, summarizing it on the Record of Evidence, writing a summary statement, determining ratings. Participants complete remaining B criteria; compare with "expert" Record of Evidence; discuss as needed. (50)	Transparency • Record of Evidence B1 "Expert" Record of Evidence, Studio Art, Domain B
LUNCH		
	b. Complete the Record of Evidence for D. The process is modeled only if necessary. Compare Records of Evidence as pairs and with the "expert" record. (45)	
15. Field Experience	Trainer reviews the purposes and expectations of the field experience; discuss as needed (10)	
END OF DAY FOUR		

DAY FIVE		
16. Making Defensible Professional Judgments (135 min)	a. Review of field experience. Participants work in pairs to examine Records of Evidence for field experience, including documentation for judgments. (60)	Record of Evidence from Field Experience
	b. Trainer explains obstacles to objectivity (halo, leniency, central tendency). Participants identify characteristics of Records of Evidence subject to these tendencies, and examine own records from the field experience. (45)	
BREAK (10 min)		
	c. Participants explore the issues involved in making complex judgments. (30)	
17. The Complete Assessment Process (195 min)	a. Participants review written materials from the H. S. Chemistry tape. (15)	Class Profile, Instruction Profile
	b. Participants watch the preobservation interview, and take notes. (10)	Video Tape
LUNCH		
	c. Participants watch the classroom lesson and take notes. They then clarify their notes. (45)	Video Tape
	d. Participants watch the postobservation conference, and take notes. (10)	Video Tape
	e. Participants code their notes from all sources to the criteria. (15)	
BREAK (10 MIN)		
	f. Participants assemble evidence from all sources for each criterion, summarize that evidence, and assign a rating. (60)	Record of Evidence
	g. Trainer distributes the "expert" record of evidence; participants identify discrepancies, discuss as needed. (40)	"expert" Record of Evidence
END OF DAY FOUR		

Appendix D

PRAXIS III: Classroom Performance Assessments

OVERVIEW

Alice Sims-Gunzenhauser
Educational Testing Service
Princeton, NJ

October 1992

Introduction

PRAXIS III: Classroom Performance Assessments of *THE PRAXIS SERIES: Professional Assessments for Beginning Teachers*™ constitute a system for assessing the skills of beginning teachers in their own classroom settings. PRAXIS III was developed by Educational Testing Service for use in teacher licensing decisions made by states or local agencies empowered to license teachers. Under the Guidelines that govern its use, PRAXIS III may *not* be used for the purpose of making employment decisions about teachers who are already licensed. PRAXIS III is intended to be an open, public system. Its framework of knowledge and skills for beginning teachers, including the assessment criteria and scoring rules, and the assessment process, should be made available to all those who are involved in the use of PRAXIS III, particularly the beginning teachers themselves. It is hoped that the criteria can become part of the growing professional dialogue among teachers, and can contribute to support programs for beginning teachers.

The PRAXIS III system uses three assessment methods—direct observation of classroom practice, review of written documentation prepared by the teacher, and semi-structured interviews. The assessment is centered around direct observation by a trained assessor of a lesson or instructional event taught by the beginning teacher. Prior to the observation, the beginning teacher provides the assessor with written documentation that conveys a sense of the general classroom context and the students in the class, as well as specific information about the lesson to be observed. Semi-structured interviews before and after the observation allow for exploration of the teacher's rationales for his or her decisions and practices. The interviews are also intended to assess the teacher's ability to relate instructional decisions to contextual factors such as student characteristics.

As used here, the term "system" refers to three components: (a) the framework of knowledge and skills for beginning teachers used in PRAXIS III to assess teaching performance, including a set of assessment criteria and accompanying scoring rules that apply to all grade levels and content areas; (b) the various instruments and forms used by trained assessors to collect data (Class Profile, Instruction Profile, Preobservation Interview, Classroom Observation Record, and Postobservation Interview), and the form used to analyze data and score the teaching performance (Record of Evidence); and (c) the training of assessors to document the teacher's performance, and to accurately and reliably interpret and score the performance assessment data.

PRAXIS III uses the term "assessment cycle" to describe the set of assessment activities centered around a single instructional event or lesson. The use of multiple assessment cycles makes it possible to assess the beginning teacher's performance in a variety of instructional circumstances. This allows the teacher to demonstrate his or her competence in using different classroom structures (e.g., whole-class instruction, small-group instruction, individualized instruction, group projects) and in teaching different content areas or different groups of students.

The Framework of Knowledge and Skills

The framework of knowledge and skills for beginning teachers used in PRAXIS III is derived from a national research base; its structure and the details of its content were shaped and refined through fieldwork and collaboration with educators in Delaware and Minnesota during 1991-92. Its philosophical basis is outlined in "Guiding Conceptions and Assessment Principles for The PRAXIS Series: Professional Assessments for Beginning Teachers ™ (Dwyer and Villegas, 1992). The framework of knowledge and skills consists of four interrelated domains—Organizing Content Knowledge for Student Learning, Creating an Environment for

Student Learning, Teaching for Student Learning, and Teacher Professionalism. Each domain consists of criteria used to assess the teacher's performance; there are a total of 19 criteria among the domains. Each criterion represents a critical aspect of teaching. The criteria are designed to allow a maximum amount of flexibility in how they may be demonstrated. Unlike assessment systems that limit attention to issues of equity and diversity to a single criterion or a small subset of these, PRAXIS III has infused a multicultural perspective throughout the system. This cultural infusion is based on the premise that effective teaching requires familiarity with students' background knowledge and experiences (including their cultural resources) and they use this familiarity to devise appropriate instruction. General descriptions of the four domains follow.

Domain A: Organizing Content Knowledge for Student Learning. Knowledge of the content to be taught underlies all aspects of good instruction. Domain A focuses on how teachers use their understanding of students and subject matter to decide on learning goals; to design or select appropriate activities and instructional materials; to sequence instruction in ways that will help students to meet short- and long-term curricular goals; and to design or select informative evaluation strategies. All of these processes, beginning with the learning goals, must be aligned with each other, and because of the diverse needs represented in any class, each of the processes mentioned must be carried out in ways that take into account the variety of knowledge and experiences that students bring to class. Therefore, knowledge of relevant information about the students themselves is an integral part of this domain.

Domain A is concerned with how the teacher thinks about the content to be taught. This thinking is evident in how the teacher organizes instruction for the benefit of her or his students. The primary sources of evidence for this domain are the Class Profile, Instruction Profile, and Preobservation Interview. The classroom observation may also contribute to assessing performance in this area.

Domain B: Creating an Environment for Student Learning. Domain B relates to the social and emotional components of learning as prerequisites to and context for academic achievement. Thus, most of the criteria in this domain focus on the human interactions in the classroom, on the connections between teachers and students, and among students. Domain B addresses issues of fairness and rapport, of helping students to believe that they can learn and can meet challenges, of establishing and maintaining constructive standards for behavior in the classroom. It also includes the learning "environment" in the most literal sense—the physical setting in which teaching and learning take place.

A learning environment that provides both emotional and physical safety for students is one in which a broad range of teaching and learning experiences can occur. Teachers must be able to use their knowledge of their students in order to interpret their students' behavior accurately and respond in ways that are appropriate and supportive. When they do so, their interactions with students consistently foster the students' sense of self-esteem. In addition, teachers' efforts to establish a sense of the classroom as a community with clear standards should never be arbitrary; all behavioral standards and teacher-student interactions should be grounded in a sense of respect for all members of the classroom community.

Evidence for the criteria in Domain B is drawn primarily from the classroom observation; supporting evidence may be drawn form both the pre- and postobservation interviews. The Class Profile provides contextual information relevant to the criteria comprising this domain.

Domain C: Teaching for Student Learning. This domain focuses on the act of teaching and its overall goal: helping students to connect with the content. As used here, "content" refers to the subject matter of a discipline and may include knowledge, skills, perceptions and values in any domain: cognitive, social, artistic, physical and so on. Teachers direct students in the process of establishing individual connections with the content, thereby devising a good "fit" for the content within the framework of the students' knowledge, interests, abilities, cultural backgrounds and personal backgrounds. At the same time, teachers should help students to move beyond the limits of their current knowledge or understanding. Teachers monitor learning, making certain that students assimilate information accurately and that they understand and can apply what they have learned. Teachers must also be sure that students understand what is expected of them procedurally during the lesson and that class time is used to good purpose.

Most of the evidence for a teacher's performance with respect to these criteria will come from the classroom observation. It may be augmented or illuminated by evidence from the pre- and postobservation interviews, the Instruction Profile, and the Class Profile.

Domain D: Teacher Professionalism. Teachers must be able to evaluate their own instructional effectiveness in order to plan specific future lessons for particular classes and to improve their teaching over time. They should be able to discuss the degree to which different aspects of a lesson were successful in terms of instructional approaches, student responses, and learning outcomes. Teachers should be able to explain how they will proceed to work toward learning for *all* students. The professional responsibilities of all teachers, including beginning teachers, also include sharing appropriate information with other professionals and with families in ways that support the learning of diverse student populations.

The primary source of evidence for the criteria in Domain D is the postobservation interview.

The Assessment Process

Administration of PRAXIS III assessments is necessarily individualized. Initially, the procedure requires matching beginning teachers and assessors. Once an assignment is made, a mutually agreeable time for the assessment set. The beginning teacher receives the necessary forms to fill out (i.e., Class Profile and Instruction Profile, which are part of each assessment cycle). The beginning teacher fills out the forms, which are available to the assessor on the day of the assessment—for example, the assessor might have arranged to pick them up at the school office. The assessor is expected to arrive early enough to have time to review the forms before meeting with the beginning teacher.

The first assessment activity that brings beginning teacher and assessor together is the preobservation interview. This should ideally be conducted in a quiet place, free of distractions. It provides a chance for the two participants to review the two profiles and for the assessor to gain more of a sense of the context of the class. If the Instruction Profile has become outdated, the beginning teacher can explain any changes in his or her plans for the lesson. The interview focuses primarily on issues that relate to the criteria in Domain A; in general, how the beginning teacher has planned and organized the lesson, how he or she becomes familiar with students' background knowledge and experiences, and how that familiarity influences planning decisions. The assessor notes in writing the beginning teacher's responses to the interview questions.

Following the preobservation interview is the actual observation, either a class period or a lesson in length. The assessor takes careful notes of what teacher and students say and do. The notes should be objective and descriptive; no judgments are being made at this point. After the observation, the assessor looks over the notes and identifies any areas that need clarification during the postobservation interview. The postobservation interview should follow shortly thereafter. In it, the beginning teacher is asked to reflect on how the lesson went both in general and for specific students, and on how he or she might adjust later instruction. The beginning teacher also has an opportunity to talk about whether he or she departed from the activities outlined on the Instruction Profile, and if so, why. The postobservation interview also includes questions that focus on how the beginning teacher builds professional relationships with colleagues and communicates with students' parents or guardians. The assessor again takes notes during the interview.

The postobservation interview completes the interactive stage of the assessment cycle. At this point, the assessor looks over all the notes taken—during the preobservation interview, observation, and postobservation interview—as well as the information on the written documents. Although there are general expectations about which phase of the assessment cycle will provide evidence for each criterion, there is always the possibility that good evidence will come from an unexpected source within the assessment cycle. The assessor sorts out what evidence there is (positive and/or negative) for each criterion, selects the most salient evidence of performance for each, and transfers it to the Record of Evidence form. After weighing the evidence for each criterion, the assessor writes a summary statement linking the evidence to the criterion's scoring rules and assigns a score for each criterion. The importance of the Record of Evidence is stressed in assessor training: it must be clear and cogent, presenting evidence to support the assigned score. This is particularly critical because of the nature of PRAXIS III decision-making; the assessor is asked to use his or her honed professional judgment to weigh potentially conflicting evidence of the beginning teacher's skill. The Record of Evidence, therefore, is a key document of the PRAXIS III system, representing the exercise of the assessor's skill in the service of providing accurate information about the beginning teacher's performance.

The scores that the beginning teacher receives for each assessment cycle are combined to reach a decision about licensure in accordance with decision rules set by the state.

Assessor Training

The assessor training program for PRAXIS III: Classroom Performance Assessments consists of a five-day experience for educators to enable them to make professionally defensible judgments regarding the classroom performance of beginning teachers. It consists of a series of structured activities in which trainees learn to recognize the presence or the absence—of each of the 19 criteria in a range of educational settings.

As part of learning to recognize the criteria in a range of contexts, assessors-in-training acquire skill in the various methods that PRAXIS III uses to collect information about teaching performance: evaluating written information provided by the teacher, taking accurate notes during classroom observation, and conducting semi-structured interviews. Participants practice each of these skills separately before applying them to the assessment process.

The training program follows the sequence used in the PRAXIS III assessment process itself. Participants begin by learning to identify the Domain A criteria, primarily through evaluation of written information about the class provided by the teacher and through the preobservation conference. This is followed by consideration of Domains B and C, those criteria that are principally observed in classroom observation. Lastly, trainees learn to identify the criteria in Domain D, which are manifested primarily through the postobservation conference.

The assessor training program utilizes different stimuli, as appropriate, for the different exercises. These include worksheets, sample records of evidence, simulations, case studies, and videotapes. As they progress through the training program, participants receive feedback on their work, from the instructor, from fellow participants, and from the answer keys to the exercises themselves. In addition, assessors engage in frequent professional reflection, through keeping a journal, in order to explore the complex issues involved in assessment of educators.

The PRAXIS III training program models the framework and criteria for the system as a whole. That is, the PRAXIS III system is grounded in an active and constructivist view of learning and teaching, in which the student's background experiences and prior knowledge are regarded as instructional resources. Similarly, the PRAXIS III training program, while it teaches participants to make legally defensible judgments, builds on the professional experiences of the trainees. Thus, many of the activities are highly experiential, and require that participants apply their own professional knowledge and experience to the assessment challenge.

Appendix E

Three developmental versions of criteria:

APPENDIX E.1

CRITERIA USED IN THE 1992 EDITION OF THE TRAINING MANUAL

(January, 1992)

Domain A. *Organizing Content Knowledge for Student Learning*

A thorough knowledge of the content to be taught is essential for good instructional planning, effective teaching, and informative evaluation of the results. Teachers must have adequate understanding of their subject matter to decide on learning goals, to design or select appropriate activities and instructional materials; to sequence instruction in ways that will help students to meet short- and long-term curricular goals; and to design informative evaluation strategies. Since all of the activities are undertaken in the service of student learning, each of them must be carried out in ways that are appropriate to the students. Knowledge of relevant information about the students themselves, therefore, is also part of this area.

A1: Articulating clear learning goals that are appropriate to the students

A2: Demonstrating an understanding of the connections between the content that was studied previously, the current content, and the content that remains to be studied in the future

A3: Becoming familiar with relevant aspects of students' prior knowledge, skills, and cultural experiences

A4: Creating or selecting appropriate instructional materials or other resources and learning activities that are appropriate to the student and are clearly related to the goals of the lesson

A5: Creating or selecting appropriate evaluation strategies that are appropriate to the students and are clearly related to the goals of the lesson

Domain B: *Teaching for student learning*

This domain relates to the connections that are developed between students and content. As used here. "content" refers to traditional academic subject matter as well as to the skills, abilities, perceptions, etc., involved in subjects such as visual and performing arts, vocational/technical education, and physical education. There are many ways through which teachers can make content comprehensible to students: teachers can provide direct instruction, they may be facilitators, or even observers in classroom setting they have structured so that students can work independently. Thus, in different ways, teachers help students establish a relationship with the content. Whatever the level and nature of students' involvement, teachers are responsible for communicating to students the belief that they can learn and can think. Teachers direct students in the process of establishing individual connections with the content, thereby devising a good "fit" for the content within the framework of their own knowledge, interests, abilities, cultural and personal backgrounds, etc. Teachers guide and monitor students in the process of assimilating the content, making certain that what is learned is factually and procedurally correct.

B1: Communicating high expectations for each student

B2: Making learning expectations clear to students

B3: Making content comprehensible to students

B4: Encouraging students to extend their thinking

B5: Monitoring students' understanding of content through a variety of means, providing feedback to students to assist learning, and adjusting learning activities as the situation demands

B6: Using instructional time effectively

Domain C: *Creating an Environment for Student Learning*

A safe, well-functioning learning environment is one in which a broad range of teaching and learning experiences can take place. A climate of shared responsibility and a sense of community foster equitable and mutually respectful relationships among students, and between students and the teacher. Teachers must be aware of students' individual differences so that they can interpret their student's behavior accurately and respond appropriately.

C1: Creating a climate that promotes equity

C2: Establishing and maintaining rapport with students in ways that are appropriate to the students' developmental needs

C3: Establishing and maintaining consistent standards of mutually respectful classroom interaction and behavior

C4: Making a physical environment safe and as conducive to learning as possible

Domain D: *Teacher Professionalism*

Teachers need to be able to evaluate their own instructional effectiveness in order to plan future lessons for particular classes and to improve their teaching in general. They should be able to discuss the degree to which different aspects of a lesson were successful in terms of instructional approaches, student responses, and learning outcomes. Teachers should be able to explain how they will proceed to work toward learning for *all* students. The professional responsibilities of teachers also include sharing appropriate information with other professionals and with families in ways that support the learning of diverse student populations.

D1: Reflecting on the extent to which the instructional goals were met and explaining how insights gained from instructional experience can be used subsequently

D2: Demonstrating a sense of efficacy and acceptance of responsibility for student learning

D3: Building professional relationships with colleagues to share teaching insights and coordinate learning activities for students

D4: Communicating with parents or guardians regarding student learning

Appendix E.2

Criteria Used in 1991 Assessor Training Manual

(July, 1991)

Domain A. *Organizing Content Knowledge for Teaching*

A thorough knowledge of the content to be taught is essential for good instructional planning, effective teaching, and informative evaluation of the results. Teachers must have adequate understanding of their subject matter to design or select appropriate activities and instructional materials; to sequence instruction in ways that will help students to meet short- and long-term curricular goals; and to design informative evaluation strategies.

Domain A concerns the teacher's understanding of content, clarity in setting goals, and skill in selecting or designing activities, instructional materials, and evaluation strategies aligned to these goals.

A1: Demonstrating application of content knowledge through accurate instruction

A2: Demonstrating an understanding of the connections between the content that was studied previously, and the current content, and the content that remains to be studied in the future

A3: Creating or selecting appropriate instructional materials/ other resources and learning activities that are clearly linked to the goals or intents of the lesson

A4: Creating or selecting appropriate evaluation strategies that are clearly linked to the goals or intents of the lesson

Domain B. *Teaching for student learning*

This domain relates to the connections that are developed between students and content. As used here, "content" refers to traditional academic subject matter as well as to the skills, abilities, perceptions, etc., involved in subjects such as visual and performing arts, vocational/technical education, and physical education. There are many ways through which teachers can make content comprehensible to students: teachers can provide direct instruction, they may be facilitators, or even observers in classroom setting they have structured so that students can work independently. Thus, in different ways, teachers help students establish a relationship with the content. Whatever the level and nature of students' involvement, teachers are responsible for directing the learners in the process of establishing individual connections with the content and thereby devising a good "fit" of the content within the framework of their own knowledge, interests, abilities, cultural and personal backgrounds, etc. The teacher guides and monitors students in the process of assimilating the content, making certain that what is learned is factually and procedurally correct.

B1: Becoming familiar with relevant aspects of students' prior knowledge, skills, experiences, and cultures

B2: Helping students activate relevant aspects of their prior knowledge, skills, experiences, and cultural resources in order to promote learning

B3: Making content comprehensible to students

B4: Monitoring students' understanding of content through a variety of means, providing feedback to students to assist learning, and adjusting learning activities as the situation demands

B5: Setting high expectations for each student, making learning expectations clear to student, and helping students accept responsibility for their own learning

B6: Encouraging students to extend their own thinking

B7: Using instructional time effectively

Domain C: *Creating an Environment for Student Learning*

A safe, well-functioning learning environment is one in which a broad range of teaching and learning experiences can take place. Learning is maximized when both teacher and students establish a sense of community in which they develop and practice classroom routines, rules, and standards of behavior. A climate of shared responsibility fosters equitable and mutually respectful relationships among students, and between students and teachers.

C1: Creating a purposeful and well-functioning learning community with convenient and well-understood classroom routines

C2: Making the physical environment as conducive to learning as possible

C3: Establishing and consistently maintaining clear standards of behavior

C4: Creating a climate that ensures equity and respect for and among students, and between students and the teacher

C5: Establishing and maintaining rapport with students in ways that are appropriate to the students' developmental levels

Domain D: *Teacher Professionalism*

Teachers need to be able to evaluate their own instructional effectiveness in order to plan future lessons for particular classes and to improve their teaching in general. They should be able to discuss the degree to which different aspects of a lesson were successful in terms of instructional approaches, student responses, and learning outcomes. Teachers should be able to explain how they will use their assessment of their instructional effectiveness on a given day to guide their planning and to improve their teaching. The professional responsibilities of teachers also include sharing appropriate information with other professionals and with families in ways that support the learning of diverse student populations.

D1: Reflecting on the extent to which the instructional goals were met

D2: Explaining how insights gained from instructional experience can be used subsequently

D3: Demonstrating acceptance of responsibility for student learning

D4: Building professional relationships with colleagues to share teaching insights and coordinate learning activities for students

D5: Communicating with families regarding student learning and, where appropriate, interacting effectively with the community

APPENDIX E.3

COMPETENCIES PRESENTED TO THE NATIONAL ADVISORY COMMITTEE

(December 1990)

Domain I: Planning for Instruction

1A. Establishes learning objectives that support broad curriculum goals

2A. Develops clear, sequential learning objectives that reflect a diversity of knowledge and skill, and are appropriate to the developmental levels and skills of students

3A. Develops plans for instructional activities that will enhance student involvement and accommodate cultural and skill-level diversity

4A. Plans for the integration of appropriate resources and learning materials, which support the learning objectives

5A. Plans for a variety of assessment techniques to evaluate student learning through both formal and informal means before, during, and following instruction

Domain II: Managing the Classroom Environment

1B. Establishes and communicates classroom procedures and policies

2B. Fosters student behavior conducive to learning

3B. Manages time to maximize learning

4B. Fosters a positive environment for learning

Domain III: Implementing Instruction

1C. Places content of lesson in context

2C. Uses instructional approaches that facilitate learning the content of the lesson

3C. Encourages all students to develop higher-order thinking skills

4C. Encourages all students' learning by recognizing and providing for their developmental levels, individual characteristics, and cultural background

5C. Communicates effectively with students

6C. Displays knowledge of content

7C. Promotes high level of student involvement in classroom tasks

8C. Monitors and responds to students' progress

Domain IV: Evaluating Student Learning and Instructional Effectiveness

1D. Evaluate student performance, records information and maintains records related to student learning

2D. Provides formal feedback regarding student performance

3D. Evaluates the effectiveness of instruction to revise plans for future instruction

Appendix F

Appendix F.1

Names and Affiliations of the Literature Review Panel Members for Effective Teaching

David Berliner
College of Education
Arizona State University, Tempe

Bob Calfee
School of Education
Stanford University

Sharon Feiman-Nemser
College of Education
Michigan State University

Sandra Hollingsworth
College of Education
Michigan State University

Jane Stallings
College of Education
Texas A&M University

Laura Wagner
Intersegmental Teaching Improvement Unit
California State Department of Education

APPENDIX F.2

NAMES AND AFFILIATIONS OF THE LITERATURE REVIEW PANEL MEMBERS FOR TEACHING IN MULTICULTURAL CLASSROOMS

Ursula Casanova
Arizona State University

Lisa Delpit
Morgan State University

Michele Foster
University of California at Davis

Asa Hilliard
Georgia State University

Jacqueline Irvine
Emory University

Gerald Mohatt
University of Alaska, Fairbanks

Luis Moll
University of Arizona

Sharon Nelson-Barber
Far West Laboratory for Educational Research
    and Development

José A. Vazquez
Hunter College - City University of New York

Appendix G

Appendix G
National Advisory Committee
December 3-5, 1990
Princeton, NJ

Mariah Banks
Mentor/Intern Program
Washington, DC

David C. Berliner
Arizona State University
Tempe, AZ

Martha K. Boyce
Charlotte Mecklenburg
    School System
Charlotte, NC

Joyce Budna
State Dept. of Public Instruction
Dover, DE

Glen W. Cutlip
National Education Association
Washington, DC

Anthony DeFazio
New York City Public School System
New York, NY

Patricia Esrael
Paul Laurence Dunbar High School
Lexington, KY

Scott Grosh
Greenway Middle School Teacher
    Center
Pittsburgh, PA

Donna Hernandez
Chamberlain Schools
Goshen, IN

Denise Kenny
Readington Twp. School System
Morris Plains, NJ

Jeanne McCumby Koelin
Cuyamaca Model Education Center
El Cajon, CA

Sharon Nelson-Barber
Far West Laboratory for Educational
    Research and Development
San Francisco, CA

Carl O'Connell
Rochester City School District
Rochester, NY

Richard L. Simms
Minnesota Board of Teaching
St. Paul, MN

Robin Taylor
State Department of Public
    Instruction
Dover, DE

Caralliene Westbrook
North Street School
Greenwich, CT

Merlin C. Wittrock
University of California
Los Angeles, CA

David Wright
Commission on Teacher
    Credentialing
Sacramento, CA

Nancy Zimpher
Ohio State University
Columbus, OH